WAGE & HOUR LAW

A Guide to the Fair Labor Standards Act
and State Wage and Hour Laws

WAGE & HOUR LAW

A GUIDE TO THE FAIR LABOR STANDARDS ACT AND STATE WAGE AND HOUR LAWS

Diane M. Pfadenhauer, SPHR, Esq.

DataMotion Publishing, LLC New York

DataMotion Publishing, LLC

1019 Fort Salonga Road, Suite 10-333

Northport, NY 11768-2209

www.datamotionpublishing.com

CONTENTS

APPENDIX 7: Minimum Paid Rest Period Requirements Under State Law for Adult Employees in Private Sector – Effective January 1, 2013

INTRODUCTION AND OVERVIEW OF THE FAIR LABOR STANDARDS ACT

The Fair Labor Standards Act (FLSA) was enacted in 1938. Considered landmark legislation at a time of great economic and political upheaval, and the subject of extensive Congressional debate, the law set forth restrictions on child labor, establishing a minimum hourly wage of 25 cents and a maximum work week of 44 hours. A mere ten pages in length, the original law was revolutionary for its time.

The FLSA generally establishes minimum wage, overtime pay, recordkeeping, and child labor standards affecting full-time and part-time workers in the private sector and in Federal, State, and local governments. The law is administered and enforced by the Wage and Hour Division of the United States Department of Labor (USDOL).

For those who are just learning about the FLSA, the law contains terms whose definitions are very specific. Understanding the meaning of these terms is often key to understanding how to apply and comply with the law.

Covered, nonexempt workers are entitled to a minimum wage of $7.25 per hour. This minimum wage became effective July 24, 2009. A minimum wage of not less than $4.25 an hour is permitted for employees under 20 years of age during their first 90 consecutive calendar days of employment with an employer. A nonexempt worker is one who is not exempt from the overtime provisions of the FLSA. That means that the worker will be entitled to the general protections of the law. Nonexempt workers must be paid overtime pay at a rate of not less than one and one-half times their regular rates of pay after 40 hours of work in a workweek.

It is important to note that the FLSA requires overtime to be paid based upon an employee's "regular rate of pay." While often this rate is considered an employee's hourly rate of pay, there are many ways that the regular rate can be determined.

Wages required by the FLSA are due on the regular payday for the pay period covered. Many state laws define when an employer is required to pay employees. Deductions made from wages for such items as cash or merchandise shortages, employer-required uniforms, and tools of the trade are not legal to the extent that they reduce the wages of employees below the minimum rate required by the FLSA or reduce the amount of overtime pay due under the FLSA. In addition, employers should be mindful that many state laws prohibit such deductions entirely or regulate them specifically.

There are a number of employment practices which the FLSA does not regulate. These include, for example, paid time off policies such as vacation, sick, personal and holidays; severance pay plans; meal and rest periods; premium compensation for weekend or holiday work; pay raises; and fringe benefits. Be mindful, however, that many states do regulate these areas.

In addition, the FLSA does not limit the number of hours in a day or days in a week an employee may be required or scheduled to work, including overtime hours, if the employee is at least 16 years old.

Coverage

The law generally applies to all employees of specific enterprises having workers engaged in interstate commerce, producing goods for interstate commerce, or handling, selling, or otherwise working on goods or materials that have been moved in or produced for interstate commerce. One employment lawyer joked that the application of this rule is often so broad that standing next to someone in an elevator is enough to bring the enterprise under the application of the law.

Interestingly, employees of firms which are not covered by the FLSA still may be subject to its minimum wage, overtime pay, recordkeeping, and child labor provisions if they are individually engaged in interstate commerce or in the production of goods for interstate commerce, or in any closely-related process or occupation directly essential to such production. For example, the United States Department of Labor notes that such employees include those who: "work in communications or transportation; regularly use the mail, telephones, or telegraph for interstate communication, or keep records of interstate transactions; handle, ship, or receive goods moving in interstate commerce; regularly cross State lines in the course of employment; or work for independent employers who contract to do clerical, custodial, maintenance, or other work for firms engaged in interstate commerce or in the production of goods for interstate commerce."

Tipped employees are covered and are those individuals engaged in occupations in which they customarily and regularly receive more than $30 a month in tips. Employers can consider tips as part of employees' wages, but they must pay at least $2.13 an hour in direct wages. If an employee's tips combined with the employer's direct wages of at least $2.13 an hour do not equal the minimum hourly wage, the employer must make up the difference. Also, employees must retain all of their tips, except to the extent that they participate in a valid tip pooling or sharing arrangement.

Exemptions

Some employees are exempt from the overtime pay provisions or both the minimum wage and overtime pay provisions. See the more detailed explanation of the exemptions in Chapter 5 - Exemptions.

Exemptions from Both Minimum Wage and Overtime Pay

- *Executive, administrative, and professional employees (including teachers and academic administrative personnel in elementary and secondary schools), outside sales employees, and employees in certain computer-related occupations;*

Employees of certain seasonal amusement or recreational establishments, employees of certain small newspapers, seamen employed on foreign vessels, employees engaged in fishing operations, and employees engaged in newspaper delivery;

- *Farmworkers employed by anyone who used no more than 500 "man-days" of farm labor in any calendar quarter of the preceding calendar year;*

- *Casual babysitters and persons employed as companions to the elderly or infirm.*

Exemptions from Overtime Pay Only

- *Certain commissioned employees of retail or service establishments; auto, truck, trailer, farm implement, boat, or aircraft sales-workers; or parts-clerks and mechanics servicing autos, trucks, or farm implements, who are employed by non-manufacturing establishments primarily engaged in selling these items to ultimate purchasers;*

- *Employees of railroads and air carriers, taxi drivers, certain employees of motor carriers, seamen on American vessels, and local delivery employees paid on approved trip rate plans;*

- *Announcers, news editors, and chief engineers of certain non-metropolitan broadcasting stations;*

- *Domestic service workers living in the employer's residence;*

- *Employees of motion picture theaters; and*

- *Farmworkers.*

Partial Exemptions from Overtime Pay

- *Partial overtime pay exemptions apply to employees engaged in certain operations on agricultural commodities and to employees of certain bulk petroleum distributors.*

- *Hospitals and residential care establishments may adopt, by agreement with their employees, a 14-day work period instead of the usual seven-day workweek if the employees are paid at least time and one-half their regular rates for hours worked over eight in a day or 80 in a 14-day work period, whichever is the greater number of overtime hours.*

- *Employees who lack a high school diploma, or who have not attained the educational level of the eighth grade, can be required to spend up to 10 hours in a workweek engaged in remedial reading or training in other basic skills without receiving time and one-half overtime pay for these hours. However, the employees must receive their normal wages for hours spent in such training and the training must not be job specific.*

- *Public agency fire departments and police departments may establish a work period ranging from seven to 28 days in which overtime need only be paid after a specified number of hours in each work period.*

Child Labor

The FLSA's child labor provisions prohibit the employment of minors during certain times of the day so as not to interfere with their academic activities and also prohibit children from working in certain occupations which are deemed to be hazardous or dangerous. The USDOL Wage and Hour Division published a new Final Rule which is considered one of the most far reaching revisions to the child labor regulations. The new rule which was effective, July 19, 2010, addresses hazardous occupations, identifies permitted occupations, and clarifies work hours and prohibition on working during school hours.

Generally, in non-farm work, the permissible jobs and hours of work, by age, are as follows:

- *Youths 18 years or older may perform any job, whether hazardous or not, for unlimited hours;*

- *Minors 16 and 17 years old may perform any nonhazardous job, for unlimited hours; and*

- *Minors 14 and 15 years old may work outside school hours in various nonmanufacturing, nonmining, nonhazardous jobs under the following conditions: no more than three hours on a school day, 18 hours in a school week, eight hours on a non-school day, or 40 hours in a non-school week. Also, work may not begin before 7:00 am, nor end after 7:00 pm, except from June 1 through Labor Day, when evening hours are extended to 9:00 pm. Under a special provision, youths 14 and 15 years old enrolled in an approved Work Experience and Career Exploration Program (WECEP) may be employed for up to 23 hours in school weeks and three hours on school days (including during school hours). In addition, academically oriented youths enrolled in an approved Work–Study Program (WSP) may be employed during school hours.*

While 14 is the minimum age for most non-farm work, at any age, minors may deliver newspapers; perform in radio, television, movie, or theatrical productions; work for parents in their solely-owned non-farm business (except in mining, manufacturing or on hazardous jobs); or gather evergreens and make evergreen wreaths.

Recordkeeping Requirements

The FLSA record keeping requirements require employers to keep records of, among other things, wages and hours worked by employees. While the records do not have to be kept in any particular form and time clocks are not required, diligent records, including the use of time recording systems can help an employer demonstrate accurately the hours worked by employees.

For employees subject to the minimum wage provisions or both the minimum wage and overtime pay provisions, the following records must be kept:

- *Personal information, including the employee's name, home address, occupation, sex, and birth date if under 19 years of age;*

- *Hour and day when the workweek begins;*

- *Total hours worked each workday and each workweek;*

- *Total daily or weekly straight-time earnings;*

- *Regular hourly pay rate for any week when overtime is worked;*

- *Total overtime pay for the workweek;*

- *Deductions from or additions to wages;*

- *Total wages paid each pay period; and*

- *Date of payment and pay period covered.*

Nursing Mothers

The Patient Protection and Affordable Care Act (PPACA), which was signed into law on March 23, 2010, amended Section 7 of the FLSA to provide an unpaid break time requirement for nursing mothers.

Under the PPACA, employers are required to provide reasonable unpaid break time for an employee to express breast milk for her nursing child for one year after the child's birth each time such employee has need to express the milk. Employers are also required to provide a place, other than a bathroom, that is shielded from view and free from intrusion from coworkers and the public, which may be used by an employee to express breast milk.

The FLSA requirement of break time for nursing mothers to express breast milk does not preempt State laws that provide greater protections to employees (for example, providing compensated break time, providing break time for exempt employees, or providing break time beyond one year after the child's birth).

Employers are required to provide a reasonable amount of break time to express milk as frequently as needed by the nursing mother. The frequency of breaks needed to express milk as well as the duration of each break will likely vary.

The location provided must be functional as a space for expressing breast milk. If the space is not dedicated to the nursing mother's use, it must be available when needed in order to meet the statutory requirement. A space temporarily created or converted into a space for expressing milk or made available when needed by the nursing mother is sufficient provided that the space is shielded from view and free from any intrusion from co-workers and the public.

It is important to note that only nonexempt employees are entitled to breaks to express milk. Employers may, however, be obligated to provide breaks to exempt employees under state law.

Employers with fewer than 50 employees are not subject to the FLSA break time requirement if compliance with the provision would impose an undue hardship. Whether compliance would be an undue hardship is determined by looking at the difficulty or expense of compliance for a specific employer in comparison to the size, financial resources, nature, and structure of the employer's business.

Computing Overtime Pay

Generally, for nonexempt employees, overtime pay must be paid at a rate of at least one and one-half times the employee's regular rate of pay for each hour worked in a workweek in excess of 40 hours in a work week. The regular rate generally includes all payments made by the employer to or on behalf of the employee (except for certain statutory exclusions).

Thus, employers are warned that this is not always the employee's hourly rate. It will include certain bonus payments. In addition, the base hourly rate will be influenced by the standard workweek and what the employer policy is with regard to determining the base rate which, of course, is subject to the law. The regular rate may not be less than the minimum wage required by the FLSA.

To add to the confusion, if a salary is paid on other than a weekly basis, the weekly pay must be determined in order to compute the regular rate and overtime pay. If the salary is for a half month, it must be multiplied by 24 and the product divided by 52 weeks to get the weekly equivalent. A monthly salary should be multiplied by 12 and the product divided by 52.

CHAPTER 1: FLSA COVERAGE

One of the first things an employer or employee must determine is whether or not the Fair Labor Standards Act (FLSA) applies to that enterprise or individual. Determining whether one is covered by the FLSA generally means determining whether the business is a covered entity or, if it is not, whether the employees are still covered employees under the Act. Generally, the United States Department of Labor (USDOL) has stated those covered by the FLSA are the employees of certain enterprises with workers engaged in interstate commerce, producing goods for interstate commerce, or handling, selling or otherwise working on goods or materials that have been moved in or produced for commerce by any person.

Covered Enterprises

A covered enterprise (covered employer) is one where related activities are performed through common control or operation by any person for a common business purpose, and:

- *The annual volume of sales made (or business done) is $500,000 or more; or*

- *The enterprise is engaged in the operation of a hospital, an institution primarily engaged in the care of sick, aged or mentally ill who reside on the premises; a school for mentally or physically disabled or gifted children; a preschool, elementary, or secondary school or an institution of higher education (whether for profit or not for profit); or*

- *The enterprise is a public agency.*

The $500,000 annual volume test was added to the FLSA when it was revised in 1990. Those enterprises that were covered prior to March 31, 1990 and then no longer covered because of the revised $500,000 test are still subject to the overtime pay, child labor, and recordkeeping provisions of the FLSA.

Covered Employees

An employee may still be subject to the overtime pay, minimum wage, recordkeeping and child labor provisions of the FLSA even if the employee works for a business or organization that is not a covered enterprise. Covered employees must be individually engaged in interstate commerce or in the production of goods for interstate commerce or in any closely related occupation essential to such production. Covered employees include those who regularly use the mail or telephone for interstate communication; work in communications or transportation; regularly cross state lines; handle, ship or receive goods moving in interstate commerce; or work for independent employers who contract to do work for firms engaged in interstate commerce or the production of goods for interstate commerce.

In addition to workers at covered enterprises and covered employees, the FLSA's provisions also cover certain domestic service workers. Domestic service workers are covered if their cash wages from one employer in a calendar year are above the threshold set, and adjusted annually, by the Social Security Administration ($1,700 in 2010), or they work a total of more than eight hours a week for one of more employers. Examples of covered domestic service workers may include housekeepers, day workers, chauffeurs, cooks or full-time babysitters.

Independent Contractor Issues

For FLSA purposes, the employer-employee relationship is determined by the economic reality of the relationship, not by common law standards relating to master and servant. Whether an employer-employee relationship exists is determined based on the facts on a case-by-case basis, and it does not matter if the parties consider the worker to be an independent contractor. The Supreme Court has stated that generally, an employee, as opposed to an independent contractor in business on his/her own, is one who "follows the usual path of an employee" and is dependent on the business that he/she serves.

There is no one rule or test for determining whether a worker is an independent contractor or employee covered by the FLSA, instead each case is viewed individually and any number of factors may be considered. Some significant factors in determining the employment relationship include:

- *The extent to which the services rendered by the worker are an essential part of the principal's business.*
- *The permanency of the relationship between the principal and worker.*
- *The investment into facilities and equipment by the supposed independent contractor.*
- *The nature and degree of control exercised by the principal.*

- *The opportunities for profit and loss by the supposed independent contractor.*

- *The amount of initiative, judgment, or foresight required for the success of the claimed independent contractor.*

- *The degree to which the supposed contractor has an independent business organization and/or operation.*

While the above factors are considered significant to use to determine whether an employment relationship exists, other factors are considered insignificant in the determination. The DOL considers the following factors immaterial to the employment relationship determination: where the work is performed, whether the claimed independent contractor is licensed by state or local government, the time and mode of pay, and the absence of a formal employment agreement. These factors are not considered to have any bearing on whether an employment relationship exists.

The DOL has identified some typical situations where the independent contractor or other employment relationship issues arise. First, the construction industry, where contractors hire claimed independent contractors who really should be considered employees because they do not meet the test for true independence from the principal. A second typical situation involves franchise arrangements where the issue is the level of control the franchisor has over the franchisee. Employees of the franchisee may actually be considered employed by the franchisor (or employed by both). Another situation employers should be wary of is one where an individual does work from his/her own home. Working from home does not automatically make the individual an independent contractor. Employers often misclassify those who work from home as independent contractors.

Joint Employers and Temporary Workers

It is important to be aware of possible joint employment issues that may arise because joint employers are responsible, both individually and jointly, for compliance with all provisions of the FLSA. A joint employment relationship is generally established where an employee performs work that benefits two or more employers at the same time, or the employee works for two or more employers during the same workweek and employment by one employer is not completely disassociated from employment by another employer.

All of the employee's work for all joint employers in one workweek is considered as one employment for FLSA purposes. Whether a joint employer relationship exists depends upon all the facts in each case; the determination is made on a case-by-case basis. An employer can satisfy the joint obligations under the FLSA by taking credit for all payments made to the employee by the other employer(s) for minimum wage and overtime requirements.

A joint employer relationship is generally found in the following situations:

- *Where there is an arrangement between two or more employers to share an employee's work or services.*

- *Where one employer acts, directly or indirectly, in the interest of another employer(s) in relation to the employee.*

- *Where employers are not completely disassociated from one another with respect to the employment of a certain employee. The employers may be deemed to share control of the employee because one employer controls the other employer.*

- *Multiple business entities that are deemed to compromise a single enterprise may be responsible for overtime pay based on the combined hours worked by employees shared among the entities comprising the one enterprise.*

If all of the relevant facts establish that two or more employers are acting independent of each other and are completely disassociated with respect to the employment of an employee who during the same workweek performs work for each employer, those employers are not considered joint employers. The employers may disregard all the work performed by the employee for other employers in determining their own responsibilities under the FLSA.

Temporary (contract) workers may be considered employees of the leasing company (temporary agency), the receiving company, or both. It is important that employers who utilize temporary workers determine whether they have entered into a joint employer relationship with the leasing company. If temporary workers are considered employees of both the leasing company and the receiving employer then both employers are jointly and individually responsible for compliance with the FLSA provisions.

CHAPTER 2: MINIMUM WAGE

The Fair Labor Standards Act (FLSA or the "Act") regulates various parts of labor and employment law. The four main parts of the Act govern minimum wage, overtime pay, child labor provisions, and recordkeeping requirements. This chapter focuses on the FLSA's provisions regarding the federal minimum wage. Readers of this guide should also check State wage and hour law because the States often provide employees with greater protections than the FLSA provides.

As of July 24, 2009, the federal minimum wage is $7.25 per hour. All non-exempt employees must be paid the federal minimum wage for the first 40 hours of work per week, with overtime paid for all hours beyond 40. The FLSA's exemptions and overtime pay requirements are discussed in chapters later in this book. Employees may be paid on a piece rate basis as long as they receive the equivalent of the required minimum wage. The FLSA permits certain individuals to be employed at wage rates below the statutory minimum wage under special certificates issued by the Department of Labor. These individuals include tipped employees, certain youths, student learners, full time students, and some disabled workers. Certain taxes may be included as wages such as social security, unemployment insurance, Federal, State, and local taxes. Employers cannot include in wages any deductions for taxes that, by law, are to be paid by the employer.

Pay Frequency and the Workweek

Employees are to be paid at least the minimum wage for all hours worked within the workweek. The FLSA does not require that workers be paid on a specific date, but wages are due on the regular payday for the pay period covered. A workweek is a period of 168 hours during seven consecutive 24-hour periods. A workweek can begin on any day of the week and at any hour of the day established by the employer. Generally, for the purposes of minimum wage and overtime pay, each workweek stands alone and there can be no averaging of two or more workweeks. Employee FLSA coverage, compliance with wage payment requirements, and the application of most exemptions are determined on a workweek basis.

Noncash Wages

Generally, under the FLSA, the reasonable cost or fair value of board, lodging, or other facilities customarily furnished by the employer for the employee's benefit may be considered part of wages when determining whether the employee has been paid the required minimum wage. The employee must receive the benefits of the facility for which he/she is charged and acceptance of the facility must be voluntary and un-coerced.

"Other facilities" may include meals at company restaurants or cafeterias or provided by hospitals, hotels or restaurants to their employees; meals, dorm rooms, and tuition furnished by a college to its student employees; housing furnished for dwelling purposes; general merchandise furnished at company stores and commissaries (articles of food, clothing and household effects). Further, "other facilities" may include fuel, electricity, water and gas furnished for the noncommercial personal use of the employee; and transportation furnished to employees between their homes and work where travel time does not constitute hours worked compensable under the Act and the transportation is not an incident of and necessary to the employment. Meals are always regarded as primarily for the benefit and convenience of the employee. In general, if an employer provides any of the above to the employee for the employee's benefit then the employer can count the fair value of these facilities toward the employee's wages.

The cost of furnishing any facilities primarily for the benefit of the employer will not be recognized as reasonable and may not be included in computing wages. Facilities primarily for the benefit of the employer include, but are not limited to:

- *Safety caps, explosives, and miner lamps (mining industry);*
- *Electric power – used for commercial production in the interest of the employer;*
- *Company police and guard protection;*
- *Taxes and insurance on the employer's buildings not used for employee lodging;*
- *Dues to the chamber of commerce or other organizations to repay subsidies given to the employer for locating his factory in a certain community;*
- *Transportation charges where transportation is an incident of and necessary to the employment (as in the case of maintenance-of-way employees of a railroad);*

- *Charges for uniform rental where the nature of the business requires the employee wear uniforms; and*

- *Medical services and hospitalization which the employer is bound to furnish under Workers' Compensation laws or similar Federal, State or local laws.*

Whether in cash or in facilities, wages are not considered paid by the employer and received by the employee unless paid finally and unconditionally (free and clear). The wage requirements of the FLSA are not met where the employee "kick-backs" directly or indirectly to the employer (or another person for the employer's benefit) the whole or part of the wage delivered to the employee. Payments by tokens, credit cards, coupons, and other similar devices are not proper mediums of payments.

Deductions and Garnishments

It is important that employers become aware of the permitted and prohibited wage deductions and garnishments under Federal, State, and local law. The FLSA provides guidance for some permitted and prohibited wage deductions and garnishments. In general, deductions for items like cash or merchandise shortages, employer required uniforms, and tools of the trade are not legal to the extent that they reduce wages below the minimum wage or reduce the amount of overtime pay due. An employer cannot avoid the FLSA's minimum wage requirements by having the employee reimburse the employer in cash for the cost of such items in lieu of deducting the cost from the employee's wages. State and local laws may restrict permissible wage deductions and garnishments further than the FLSA.

The FLSA does not allow uniforms or other items considered primarily for the benefit or convenience of the employer to be included as wages. An employer may not take credit for such items in meeting his/her obligations toward minimum wage or overtime pay. If wearing a uniform is required by law, the nature of the business, or an employer, the cost and maintenance of the uniform is considered to be a business expense of the employer. If an employer requires employees to bear this cost it may not reduce the employee's wage below the minimum wage or cut into the employee's overtime pay. For example, an employee who is paid $7.25 per hour (the federal minimum wage) cannot be required to purchase his/her own uniform or have the cost deducted from his/her pay. However, if that employee earns $7.75 per hour for 30 hours then the maximum the employer could legally deduct is $15 ($0.50 x 30). An employer may prorate deductions over a period of paydays provided the prorated deductions do not reduce the employee's wages below the required minimum wage in any workweek.

Employers sometimes require employees to pay for items other than uniforms. The cost of any items primarily for the benefit or convenience of the employer would have the same restrictions as those applied to reimbursement for uniform costs. No deductions may be made that reduce an employee's earnings below the required minimum wage. Some items

---

considered primarily for the benefit or convenience of the employer include tools used in the employee's work, damages to the employer's property by the employee or any other individual, financial loss due to clients/customers not paying bills, and theft of the employer's property by the employee or other individuals.

A wage garnishment is any legal procedure through which some portion of a person's earnings is required to be withheld by an employer for the payment of a debt. Most garnishments are made by court order, and other types include Internal Revenue Service or State tax collection agency levies for unpaid taxes and federal agency administrative garnishments for non-tax debts owed to the federal government. Wage garnishments do not include voluntary wage assignments by the employee.

Title III of the Consumer Credit Protection Act (CCPA) limits the amount of an employee's earnings that may be garnished and protects employees from being fired if their pay is garnished for only one debt. The CCPA prohibits an employer from firing an employee whose wages are garnished for one debt, but there is no prohibition against discharging an employee whose earnings are separately garnished for two or more debts. The protection applies to anyone receiving personal earnings from wages, salaries, commissions, bonuses and other sources of income including from a pension or retirement program. Tips are not considered earnings for the purpose of wage garnishment law.

The amount of pay subject to garnishment is based on the employee's disposable earnings – that is, the amount left after legally required deductions are made. Voluntary deductions, those not required by law, are not subtracted from gross earnings when calculating disposable earnings under the CCPA. The law sets the maximum amount that may be garnished in any workweek or pay period regardless of the number of garnishment orders received by the employer. If the court order is for child support or alimony then the employee's wages can be garnished up to 50% if the employee is supporting another spouse or child and 60% if not. If the garnishment is for any other reason then the employee's wages may be garnished the lesser of two figures: 25% of the employee's disposable earnings or the amount of earnings greater than 30 times the federal minimum wage (currently $217.50). If state garnishment law differs, the law resulting in the smaller garnishment must be observed. If an individual's earnings for a period are equal to or less than 30 times the minimum wage then the individual's wages may not be garnished in any amount. There is no restriction on the amount which can be withheld from an employee's disposable earnings for a State or Federal tax debt or an order of any Bankruptcy Court in a Chapter 13 bankruptcy proceeding.

Tipped Employees

According to the Act, tipped employees are those who "customarily and regularly" earn more than $30 per month in tips. Customarily and regularly means the frequency must be more than occasional, but may be less than constant. The FLSA allows employers to take a tip credit against the federal minimum wage requirement for all employees considered "tipped employees." The employee must retain all of his/her tips, and the employer is prohibited from using the tips for any reason other than determining the tip credit for the Act's purposes or for a valid tip pool.

Employers must pay tipped employees a direct wage of at least $2.13 per hour and can use the employee's tips as a credit toward the rest of the required minimum wage, $7.25 per hour. If $2.13 per hour plus the employee's tips does not equal the federal minimum wage then the employer is required to make up the difference in pay to the employee. The employee must earn at least the federal minimum wage when the employee's direct wage and tip credit are added together. Some states also have minimum wage laws specific to tipped employees. When an employee is subject to both federal and state wage laws the employee is entitled to be protected by the provisions of each law which provide the greatest benefits.

An employer who elects to use the tip credit offered by the FLSA must inform the employee in advance that the credit will be used, and the employer must be able to show that the employee receives at least the federal minimum wage when the tip credit allowance and direct wages are combined. Each employee's individual tips are controlling when determining whether the tip credit can be used. It does not matter if other employees receive more than $30 per month in tips regularly; each individual must meet the requirements in order for the tip credit to be applied to that individual's wages.

An employee must retain all of his/her tips except to the extent they participate in a valid tip sharing or tip pooling arrangement. An employer must notify employees of the tip pooling policy and any required tip pool contribution amount. Employers may only take a tip credit for the amount of tips each employee ultimately receives, and employers cannot retain any of an employee's tips for any other person. Some employees engage in tip splitting. An example of tip splitting is where waiters give a portion of their tips to busboys. In the case of tip splitting, both the amounts retained by each employee (ex. the waiters and busboys) are considered the tips of the individuals who retain them.

The Act's regulations provide some description of what are not received tips, and employers cannot consider these "payments" as part of the tip credit allowance when calculating a tipped employee's wages. A compulsory charge for service; for example, 15% of the amount of the bill, imposed on a customer by an employer's establishment is not a tip. Even if the charge is distributed to employees it cannot be counted as a tip received in applying the tip credit. Additionally, where a hotel negotiates with a banquet facilities' customer any charged amounts included for distribution to employees of the hotel are not counted as tips received. Service charges and other similar sums that become part of the employer's gross receipts are not tips for purposes of the Act. Further, theater tickets, passes, or other merchandise received by employees are not counted as tips received for the purposes of the FLSA.

Some employees may be employed in dual jobs. For example, a hotel maintenance man may also be a waiter in the hotel. If the employee customarily and regularly receives $30 per month in tips for the work as a waiter then he is a tipped employee only with respect to his employment as a waiter. The hours he works as a maintenance man are not subject to the tip credit, and he must be paid at least the federal minimum wage for those hours worked.

Youth Minimum Wage

One of the main areas regulated by the FLSA is child labor law; many child labor provisions are discussed in detail in Chapters 9 and 10 - Youth Provisions – Non-Agricultural Jobs and Youth Provisions – Agricultural Jobs. The FLSA provides an exception to the federal minimum wage for certain youth workers. Employers can pay workers under 20 years old a minimum wage of not less than $4.25 per hour during the first 90 consecutive calendar days of employment. After 90 days, or if the employee reaches the age of 20, the employer must pay the employee the federal minimum wage, $7.25 per hour. Employers are prohibited from displacing any employee to hire someone at the youth minimum wage.

Student Learner Minimum Wage

The FLSA allows certain student learners (vocational education students) to be paid less than the federal minimum wage. The FLSA's Student Learner Program is a program for high school students at least 16 years old who are enrolled in vocational education courses (shop classes). Employers that hire Student Learners can obtain a certificate from the Department of Labor which allows the student to be paid not less than 75% of the minimum wage rate for as long as the student is enrolled in the vocational education program. Employers must also abide by all other child labor laws.

Full-Time Student Minimum Wage

The Full-Time Student Program allows certain full-time student workers to be paid less than the federal minimum wage. This minimum wage exception applies to full-time students employed in retail or service stores, agriculture, or at colleges and universities. An employer that hires a full-time student can obtain a certificate from the Department of Labor which allows the student to be paid not less than 85% of the federal minimum wage. The certificate limits the hours that a student can work to eight hours per day and no more than 20 hours per week when school is in session and 40 hours per week when school is out. The certificate also requires an employer to abide by all other child labor laws. If at any time the student worker graduates or leaves school permanently, he/she must be paid the minimum wage.

FLSA Section 14(c)

Section 14(c) of the FLSA allows for a special minimum wage to be paid to certain workers with disabilities. Section 14(c) allows an employer to pay wages below the minimum wage to certain workers with disabilities for the job being performed. The employer must first receive certification from the Department of Labor that the special minimum wage can be paid to the employees. The certificate allows the payment of wages less than the prevailing wage to workers with disabilities for the work being performed on contracts subject to the McNamara-O'Hara Service Act (SCA) and the Walsh-Healy Public Contracts Act (PCA).

Section 14(c) does not apply unless the worker's disability actually impairs the worker's earning or productive capacity for the work being performed. The fact that a worker has a disability is not in and of itself sufficient to warrant the payment of a special minimum wage. The worker's earning or productive capacity must be impaired by a physical or mental disability, including those relating to age or injury. The FLSA's regulations provide a non-exhaustive list of some disabilities which may affect productive capacity including blindness, mental illness, mental retardation, cerebral palsy, alcoholism, and drug addiction. The regulations also provide a list of some impairments which, taken by themselves, are not considered disabilities for the purposes of paying a special minimum wage including education disabilities, chronic unemployment, receipt of welfare benefits, nonattendance at school, juvenile delinquency, and correctional parole or probation.

In order to pay workers a special minimum wage the employer must first meet all requirements imposed by the Wage and Hour Division of the Department of Labor. Employers must submit a properly completed application and the required supporting documentation to the Department of Labor. Once an employer receives the authorizing certificate, the employer may pay the special minimum wages to employees who have disabilities for the work being performed. Each worker, and, if applicable, the parent or guardian of the worker, must be informed by the employer of the terms of the certificate under which the worker is employed. The employer must provide this information both orally and in writing. Certificates covering employees of work centers and patient workers normally remain in effect for two years. Certificates covering workers with disabilities placed in competitive employment situations or School Work Exploration Programs (SWEPs) are issued annually.

There is no one set special minimum wage for workers certified under Section 14(c). Instead the workers are paid commensurate wage rates based on the worker's individual productivity, no matter how limited, in proportion to the wage and productivity of experienced workers who do not have disabilities performing essentially the same type, quality, and quantity of work in the geographic area from which the labor force of the community is taken. There are three key elements used in determining the commensurate wage rates. First, the standard for workers who do not have disabilities must be determined because this is the objective gauge against which the productivity of the worker with a disability is measured. The prevailing wage must also be determined. This is the wage paid to experienced workers who do not have disabilities for the same or similar work, and who are performing such work in the area. Most SCA contracts include a wage determination specifying the prevailing wage rates to be paid for work on the SCA contract. Then the quantity and quality of the productivity of the worker with the disability must be evaluated. All special minimum wages must be reviewed and adjusted, if appropriate, at periodic intervals. At a minimum, the productivity of hourly paid workers must be reevaluated every six months, and a new prevailing wage survey must be conducted at least every twelve months.

CHAPTER 3: HOURS WORKED

Under the Fair Labor Standards Act, employees must be paid for all the time considered hours worked, and all hours worked must be counted when determining overtime pay. The amount of pay due an employee cannot be determined without knowing the total number of hours actually worked by that employee in each workweek.

The Act includes in the definition of employ "to suffer or permit to work." This means that work not requested but suffered or permitted is time that must be paid. An employee's hours worked includes all time the employee is necessarily required to be on the employer's premises, on duty, or at a prescribed work place. Additionally, if an employee volunteers to continue after his/her shift ends, those hours are also compensable. Generally, any work that is suffered or permitted must be counted as hours worked. This applies to work away from the employer's premises or job site, or even work at home. If the employer knows or has reason to believe work is being done, he/she must count that time as hours worked.

Timekeeping

The Act permits employers to use any timekeeping method they choose. Permissible timekeeping methods include time clocks, a timekeeper to keep track of employees' work hours, and telling workers to write their own times on their records. Any timekeeping plan is acceptable as long as it is complete and accurate.

If employees work on fixed schedules that rarely vary, an employer may keep a record of the exact schedule of daily and weekly hours and just indicate that the employee followed the schedule for a particular workweek. This is considered a complete and accurate timekeeping record. When the worker is on the job for longer or shorter periods than the schedule shows then the employer must record the number of hours actually worked, on an exception basis.

Commuting Time

Generally, ordinary home to work travel is not work time. An employee who travels from home before the regular workday and returns home at the end of the workday is engaged in ordinary home to work travel. This commuting time is a normal incident of employment and is not working time. Home to work travel may be working time in some instances when it is an emergency situation. For instance, if an employee is called at night, after going home at the end of the day, and the employee must travel a substantial distance to perform an emergency job for one of the employer's customers then all of the time spent is working time.

On some occasions, an employer may require employees travel to another city on a one-day assignment. Time spent traveling to and returning from the other city is work time. However, the employer may deduct (or not count) that time the employee would normally spend commuting to the regular site.

Travel Time

Travel time may or may not be considered working time depending on the kind of travel involved.

The Portal-to-Portal Act eliminates from working time certain travel time and other similar preliminary and concluding activities performed prior or subsequent to the workday, which are not included as compensation by contract, custom or practice. Preliminary and concluding activities are those that do not include the principal act. The Portal-to-Portal Act does not affect the computation of hours worked within the workday. It only affects those activities done before or after the workday. The workday is generally the period between the time the employee commences his/her principal activities and the time he/she ceases such activities. A workday may be longer than the employee's scheduled shift, hours, tour of duty, or time on the production line. Each workday's duration may vary from day to day.

Travel that is all in a day's work is work time which must be counted as hours worked. This means that any time spent by an employee in travel as part of the principal activity of the job is hours worked. Such travel includes travel from job site to job site during the workday.

Travel that keeps an employee away overnight is travel away from home. This time is clearly working time when it overlaps with the employee's workday. Any hours worked on regular working days during normal working hours are compensable hours worked, but also included are hours on nonworking days during corresponding hours to normal workdays. Travel time outside of regular working hours is not included when the employee is a passenger on a plane, train, bus or automobile. Any work performed while traveling on the employer's behalf must be paid as hours worked.

Nonproductive Time

Nonproductive time includes waiting time, travel time, on call time, and any other hours worked when the employee is not actually being productive for the employer. There cannot be an agreement between an employer and employee that the employee will only be paid for productive time. However, the Act allows for a wage agreement between the employer and employee which establishes the employee will be paid at a lower rate (at least minimum wage) for compensable nonproductive work time. Any time designated as nonproductive time must be clearly, carefully, and exactly recorded. In these instances, the employee's regular rate is the weighted average of the two rates. Without a wage agreement the employee must be paid the same rate for all time.

Nonproductive time can also count as working time without a special hourly rate assigned because the parties agree that the other compensation received by the employee is intended to cover the pay for such nonproductive hours. An example of this would be a pieceworker who agrees with the employer that the pay the employee earns at the set piece rate is intended to compensate for all the hours worked, both productive and nonproductive. The regular rate is determined by dividing the total piecework earnings by the total hours worked, productive and nonproductive, in the workweek. The rate must be equal to at least the minimum wage and overtime is due for any hours worked beyond 40 in the workweek.

Waiting Time

Whether or not waiting time is hours worked depends upon the particular circumstances of the situation. The facts may show that an employee was engaged to wait, which would be work time or that the employee is waiting to be engaged, which is not work time. The determination whether waiting time is work time, and therefore hours worked, involves scrutiny of any agreement between the parties and the practical construction of the working relationship. The conduct, nature of the service being considered and its relation to the waiting time must be scrutinized, along with all other circumstances of the situation.

An example of someone who is on duty during waiting time is a stenographer who reads while waiting for dictation. The stenographer's reading time would be hours worked. Other examples of work where waiting time is also working time is a messenger who works on a crossword puzzle while waiting for assignments or firemen playing checkers while waiting for alarms. The employees in these examples are unable to use the time effectively for their own purposes. The time belongs to and is controlled by the employer, and waiting is an integral part of the jobs.

Waiting time is not working time when an employee is completely relieved from duty and the time periods are long enough to enable the employee to use the time effectively for his/

her own purposes. An employee is not relieved from duty or able to use the time effectively unless he/she is definitively told in advance that he/she may leave the job and will not have to commence work until a specified hour has arrived. Whether the time period is long enough to enable to the employee to use the time effectively depends on all the facts and circumstances of the situation.

On Call Time

An employee who is required to remain on call on the employer's premises or so close to it that the employee cannot use the time effectively for his/her own purposes is working while on call. That time must be included in the employee's hours worked. However, it is not working time if the employee only has to leave word at home or with the company where the employee can be reached while on call.

Preparatory and Concluding Activities

Certain preparatory or concluding activities performed by employees may be considered working time. The activities will be considered hours worked if they are integral parts of the principal activity of the employee's occupation. An integral part of the employee's principal activity is an activity which is indispensable to its performance. For example, cleaning, oiling, greasing or installing a new cutting tool on the employee's work machine is an integral part of the employee's principal activity. Similarly, donning and doffing a specific uniform because the employee works in a chemical plant would be an integral part of the employee's principal activity. However, simply changing clothes at the beginning or end of a shift is not an integral part of every job. If changing clothes is just a convenience to the employee and not directly related to his/her principal activities it is not considered working time.

Some activities which have been held to be integral parts of an employee's principal activity include changing clothes and showering at a battery plant where the manufacturing involves extensive use of caustic and toxic materials; or knifemen in a meatpacking plant sharpening their knives before and after the scheduled workday. Checking in and out or waiting on line to do so are not ordinarily considered integral parts of the employee's principal act.

Living on Premises and Homeworkers

Employees who reside on the employer's premises on a permanent or extended basis, or who work from their own home, do not need to be paid for all the time they are on the premises. All of the time is not considered working time simply because they live on the premises or work from their homes. Employees may engage in normal private pursuits and have enough time to eat, sleep, entertain, and take part in other activities when they are free from all of their duties and may leave the premises for their own purposes. Since it is more difficult to determine an employee's exact hours worked under these circumstances, any reasonable agreement between the employer and employees will be considered acceptable by the Department of Labor as long as the agreement takes into account all the pertinent facts of the situation.

Employers must be careful to include as hours worked proper preparatory and concluding activities, travel, and training time for homeworkers.

Rest and Meal Periods

Whether or not a rest or meal period is considered working time and must be paid as hours worked depends on the length of the period and the specific situation. In general, rest periods of short duration, 20 minutes or less, are common and customarily paid for as working time. Short rest periods must be counted as hours worked. However, unauthorized extensions of authorized work breaks do not need to be counted as hours worked when the employer has expressly and unambiguously communicated to the employee that the authorized break may only last for a specific length of time and that any extension is contrary to the employer's rules and will be punished.

Bona fide meal periods generally do not need to be compensated as work time. A bona fide meal period is typically 30 minutes or more, although a shorter period may be recognized as a bona fide meal period under special conditions. An employee must be completely relieved from duty for the purpose of eating regular meals in order for the time to be considered nonworking time. An employee is not relieved of all duties if he/she is required to perform any duties, whether active or inactive, while eating. An employee who eats at his/her desk during the meal period, answers phones and refers callers is working and is not on a bona fide meal break. It is not necessary that an employee be permitted to leave the employer's premises as long as the employee is otherwise freed from all duties during the meal period.

Sleep Time

There are different rules for determining whether or not sleep time is work time depending on whether or not the employee is on duty for fewer than 24 hours or 24 hours or more.

An employee who is on duty for fewer than 24 hours is working even though he/she is permitted to sleep or engage in other activities when it is not busy. All hours must be paid as hours worked. For example, an operator who is on duty is working even though he/she is permitted to sleep when not busy answering phone calls. The hours are counted as hours worked even if the employee is provided sleeping facilities because the time is given to the employer and the employee is required to be on duty so the time is working time.

Employees who are scheduled to work 24 hours or more can agree with their employer to a bona fide regularly scheduled sleeping period which will not be counted as working time. Not more than eight hours may be excluded from hours worked even if the employee sleeps for longer. The employer must provide adequate sleeping facilities to employees in order to deduct sleeping time from hours worked, and the employee must usually be able to enjoy an uninterrupted night's sleep. No deduction from hours worked is permitted unless the employee is able to sleep for at least five hours during the scheduled sleep period. When there is no express or implied agreement between employees and the employer, sleeping time constitutes hours worked, even if the employer provides sleeping facilities and eight hours of sleep time.

If a bona fide sleeping period is interrupted by a call to duty, the interruption must be counted as hours worked. Additionally, if the sleeping period is interrupted to such an extent that the employee cannot get a reasonable night's sleep, the entire period must be counted as hours worked.

Training Time

Employee training time may or may not be considered hours worked depending upon the circumstances surrounding the training. Lectures, meetings, and training programs are not working time if they are outside of the employee's regular working hours, are attended voluntarily, are not directly related to the employee's job, and the employee does not perform any productive work during such attendance. Training is not voluntary if the employer requires it, even if the employee is free to choose when to attend the training. Additionally, training attendance will not be considered voluntary if the employee is led to believe that his/her present working conditions or continuance of employment will be adversely affected by non-attendance.

Training is considered working time if it is directly related to the employee's job. Training is directly related to a job if it is designed to make the employee handle his/her job more effectively, as distinguished from training the employee for another job or in a new or additional skill. A training course designed for the bona fide purpose of preparing the employee for advancement by upgrading his/her to a higher skill level and which is not designed to make the employee more efficient in his/her current job is not considered directly related to the employee's job even if the course incidentally improves the employee's skill in doing his/her regular work. Further, an employee who attends an independent school, college, or other trade school on his/her own initiative after normal work hours will not be compensated for the training time even if the courses are directly related to his/her job.

Miscellaneous Time

Adjusting Grievances

Generally, time spent adjusting grievances between an employer and employees during time the employees are required to be on the premises are hours worked. However, if there is a bona fide union involved with representing employees then the counting of such time will be determined during the collective bargaining process or by the custom or practice under a collective bargaining agreement. The Department of Labor will not determine whether or not such time should be counted as hours worked if there is a valid collective bargaining agreement which makes the determination or sets out the process for making such determination.

Medical Attention

Any time spent waiting for and receiving medical attention on the work premises or at the direction of the employer during the employee's normal working hours on work days constitutes hours worked. It will not be hours worked if the employee seeks medical attention on his/her own accord or outside of working hours.

Charitable and Civic Work

Charitable and civic work will constitute hours worked if performed at the employer's request or under his direction or control. It will also count as hours worked if the employee is required to be on the premises performing the charitable work. Time an employee spends voluntarily performing charitable and civic work, outside of the employee's normal working hours, is not hours worked.

CHAPTER 4: OVERTIME

The Fair Labor Standards Act sets the rules for overtime pay. Generally, an employer who requires or permits an employee to work overtime is required to pay the employee premium pay for the overtime worked. Unless specifically exempted, an employee covered by the Act must be paid overtime for any hours worked in excess of 40 hours in a workweek, and there is no limit to the number of hours an employee, aged 16 and over, can work in a workweek. Overtime premium pay is not required for work on Saturdays, Sundays, holidays, or regular days of rest; it is only required for hours worked over 40 in a workweek. The overtime rate must be not less than one and one-half times the employee's regular rate of pay, and the regular rate of pay must be at least the required minimum wage. Overtime pay earned in a particular workweek must be paid on the regular payday for the pay period in which the wages were earned.

Overtime pay may not be waived by an agreement between the employer and employee. An agreement that only eight hours in a day or only 40 hours in a week will count as working time also fails the test of FLSA compliance. An announcement by the employer that no overtime work will be permitted or that overtime work will not be paid for unless authorized in advance will not impair the employee's right to compensation for compensable overtime hours that are worked. Joint employers are responsible, jointly and individually, for all overtime owed to employees. The total hours worked by employees for all joint employers are added together to determine the total hours worked.

The Workweek

Overtime is evaluated on a workweek basis. A workweek is a fixed and regularly recurring period of 168 hours, in seven consecutive 24-hour periods. An employer may establish different workweeks for different employees or groups of employees. Once the beginning time of an employee's workweek is established it remains fixed regardless of the hours the employee is scheduled to work. However, the beginning of the workweek may be changed if the change is intended to be permanent and is not designed to evade the overtime requirements of the Act.

When an employer wants to change the workweek of an employee or group of employees there will be some overlap between the last workweek in the old schedule and the first workweek of the new schedule. In other words, certain hours will be within both workweeks. If the hours in both workweeks are hours in which the employee (or group of employees) does no work then his/her statutory compensation for each workweek is determined as if no overlap existed. If, however, some of the employee's work time falls within hours which are included in both workweeks the employee's straight time and overtime compensation should be computed by counting such work time as hours worked in whichever of the two workweeks its inclusion will yield the higher total compensation for both workweeks. The employee is given the benefit of having the hours counted in whichever workweek will provide the employee with the higher total compensation.

Regular Rate

Overtime premium pay must be paid at a rate of at least one and one-half times the employee's regular rate of pay. In the case of hourly employees, it is simple to determine their overtime rate of pay by multiplying the hourly rate by one and one-half. However, not all employees are paid strictly on an hourly basis. Earnings may be determined on a piece rate, salary, commission, or some other basis, but in all cases the overtime pay must be computed on the basis of the average hourly rate derived from all such earnings. When noncash payments are made to employees in the form of goods or facilities, the reasonable cost to the employer or the fair value of such goods or facilities must be included in the regular rate. The overtime rate is calculated by dividing the total pay for employment in any workweek by the total number of hours actually worked. For an employee who in a single workweek works at two or more different types of work for which different straight time rates have been established the regular rate for the week is the weighted average of such rates. The earnings from all rates are added together and divided by the total number of hours worked at all jobs.

Regular Rate Exclusions

Certain payments are not considered part of an employee's regular rate. These excluded payments include pay for expenses incurred on the employer's behalf; premium pay for overtime or true premiums paid for work on Saturdays, Sundays, and holidays; discretionary bonuses; gifts and payments in the nature of gifts on special occasions; payments for occasional periods when no work is performed due to vacation, holiday, or illness; and similar payments to an employee which are not made as compensation for the employee's employment. In the case of gifts, in order to be excluded from the employee's total earnings used to determine the regular rate they cannot be measured or dependent on the number of hours worked or the employee's production or efficiency. Other payments which may be excluded from the employee's regular rate include payments for traveling expenses, uniform laundering, buying supplies or materials on behalf of the employer, or other expenses an employee incurs while furthering the employer's interests, and which are properly reimbursable by the employer. Contributions made by an employer to a trustee or third person according to a bona fide plan for providing old age, retirement, life, accident, or health insurance or similar benefits to employees are not considered part of the regular rate. Any value or income derived from employer-provided grants or rights provided through a stock option, stock appreciation rights, or bona fide employee stock purchase program (which also meet criteria set forth in the Act's regulations) are not included in an employee's regular rate.

Sums paid in recognition of services performed by an employee during a given period are only excluded from the regular rate if one of the following three conditions is met:

- *Both the fact that the payment is made and the amount of the payment are at the sole discretion of the employer at or near the end of the period and not according to any prior contract agreement or promise causing an employee to expect such payments regularly; or*

- *The payments are made pursuant to a bona fide profit-sharing plan or trust or bona fide thrift savings plan (which meet additional requirements set forth in the Act's regulations); or*

- *Payments are talent fees paid to performers including announcers on radio and television programs.*

Certain extra compensation paid at a "premium rate" is not included in the regular rate computation, but the payments may be creditable toward overtime compensation. This extra compensation includes:

- *Premium rate payments for certain hours worked by an employee because such hours are in excess of eight in a day or 40 in the week, or in excess of the employee's normal or regular working hours.*

- *Premium rate payments for work by an employee on Saturdays, Sundays, holidays, regular days of rest, or on the sixth or seventh day of the workweek. The premium rate may not be less than one and one-half times the rate established in good faith for work performed in non-overtime hours on other days.*

- *Premium rate payments provided under an applicable employment contract or collective bargaining agreement for work outside of hours established in good faith by the contract or agreement as the basic, normal, or regular workday (not exceeding eight hours) or workweek (not exceeding 40 hours). The premium rate may not be less than one and one-half times the rate established in good faith by the contract or agreement for like work performed during the workday or workweek.*

Calculating Overtime Pay

In no case may the regular rate fall below the minimum wage required by the FLSA. Below are various examples of how to calculate the regular rate and overtime pay for employees compensated in various manners.

One Hourly Rate

Where an employee is paid one hourly rate, and no other payments are made to the employee which can be included in the regular rate, the employee's overtime pay rate is equal to one and one-half times the hourly rate. For example, an employee paid a regular rate of $8.50 per hour would have an overtime pay rate of $12.75 per hour ($8.50 x 1.5).

Commissions

Commissions paid to a non-exempt employee are included in the employee's regular rate for the purposes of determining the employee's overtime pay rate. An employee who is paid $12 per hour and $260 per week in commissions for a 40-hour workweek would have a regular rate of $18.50 per hour ($12 + $260/40). The employee's overtime pay rate is one and one-half times the regular rate or $27.75 for all overtime hours. An employer who incorrectly calculates overtime pay at a rate of $18 per hour (one and one-half times $12) will be liable for violating the FLSA by not providing proper overtime compensation to non-exempt commissioned employees.

Piece Rate

In order to determine the regular rate for piece rate workers, their total earnings are divided by the actual hours worked for the week. For example, an employee paid on a piecework basis earns $337.50 in a week and works 45 total hours. The employee's regular rate is $337.50 divided by 45 hours ($7.50 per hour). The employee's overtime rate is one and one-half times $7.50 per hour which equals $11.25 per hour. The employee in this example would be owed an additional $3.75 per hour (one-half the regular rate) for the five hours over 40 worked that week since the employee has already been paid the straight time rate for those hours. The employee's total earnings including overtime pay should be $356.25 for the week.

Salary

Generally, a non-exempt salaried employee must be paid overtime for hours worked over 40 in a week. If a salaried employee is paid a salary meant to cover only 40 hours per week then the employee's salary is divided by 40 and multiplied by one and one-half to determine that employee's overtime pay rate. For example, an employee paid $300 per week for 40 hours of work has a regular rate of $7.50 per hour. If that employee works overtime the overtime pay rate is $11.25 per hour.

However, some salaried employees are paid the same salary regardless of the number of hours worked, in which case the employee's regular rate will vary depending on the number of hours worked each week. The regular rate may never drop below the statutorily required minimum wage. For example, an employee is paid $510 per week regardless of the number of hours worked. If the employee works 50 hours one week then the regular rate equals $10.20 per hour. An additional $5.10 per hour (half the regular rate) is due for the ten hours over 40 worked, so the employee is owed $561 total for the week. If the same employee works 60 hours the next week then the regular rate for that week is $8.50 per hour and the employee is owed an additional $4.25 per hour for the 20 overtime hours. The employee is owed a total of $595 for the week.

If an employee is paid a salary on other than a weekly basis then the weekly pay must be determined in order to compute the regular rate and overtime pay. For example, if the salary is paid for one-half of a month then it must be multiplied by 24 and divided by 52 weeks in order to determine the employee's weekly pay. If the employee is paid a monthly salary then the salary should be multiplied by 12 and divided by 52 weeks to determine the weekly salary.

Multiple Hourly Rates

An employee may, during the same workweek, perform two or more different types of work at different straight time rates. The regular rate can be determined by averaging all such rates; this is done by adding the earnings from all rates together and dividing the total by the total number of hours worked at all jobs. For example, an employee who works 45 hours at a rate of $10 per hour and ten hours at $8 per hour earns a total of $530 straight time pay. The regular rate is determined by adding the earnings together and dividing by the total number of hours worked ($530 divided by 55) which results in $9.64 per hour. The employee is owed half time ($4.82 per hour) for the 15 overtime hours worked since straight time has already been paid for all hours. The employee is owed an additional $72.30 for total compensation of $602.30. Under certain conditions, the FLSA allows for the overtime pay to be based on one and one-half times the rate in effect when the overtime work is performed.

Compensatory Time

Compensatory time or "comp time" is paid time off that is earned and accrued by an employee instead of immediate cash payment for working overtime hours. The overtime requirement of the FLSA cannot be met through the use of compensatory time off except under special circumstances applicable only to a public agency that is a state, a political subdivision of a state, or an interstate governmental agency (public employees). Compensatory time is generally impermissible in the private sector.

For public employers who are allowed to utilize compensatory time, it must be paid at a rate of one and one-half times. For example, an employee who works six hours of overtime must be given nine hours of compensatory time to use. Non-public safety personnel are limited to a total of 240 compensatory hours before cash must be paid for overtime. Public safety personnel are limited to 480 hours of compensatory time before they must be paid cash for overtime worked.

Fluctuating Workweek

Some non-exempt salaried employees have hours that fluctuate from week to week. Employers are permitted to pay an employee the same salary each week as straight time for whatever hours are worked as long as certain conditions are met. The employer and employee must have a clear understanding that the salary the employee will receive is a fixed amount of straight time pay for whatever hours are worked in the workweek, however few or many. Additionally, the amount of the salary must be sufficient to provide at least the minimum wage no matter how many hours are worked. The employee's regular rate will vary from week to week depending on the total number of hours worked (see the example earlier in this chapter in the Section "Calculating Overtime Pay"). The employee's regular rate is determined by dividing the total number of hours worked into the salary paid. During overtime weeks the employee must be paid an additional one-half times the regular rate for the overtime hours. The payment for overtime hours at one-half the regular rate in addition to the salary satisfies the overtime pay requirement because the hours are already compensated at the straight time regular rate under the salary arrangement.

Piece Rates and Day Rates

Employees paid on a piece rate basis are paid a fixed amount per each item produced. Since the FLSA determines the regular rate on an hourly basis, a piece rate employee's regular rate and overtime pay rate must be computed into an hourly rate. The amount earned from piece rates and all other sources are added together and divided by the number of hours actually worked by the employee in order to determine the regular rate. An employer only needs to pay half time pay for overtime hours worked if the employee has already received straight time compensation at piece rates or by supplementary payments for all hours worked.

Piece rate employees may agree, in advance, with the employer that the employees will be paid at a rate of not less than one and one-half times the piece rate for each piece produced during overtime hours. No additional overtime pay will be due if the following conditions are met:

- *The piece rate is a bona fide rate;*

- *The overtime hours for which the overtime rate is paid qualify as overtime hours under the Act;*

- *The number of hours for which such overtime piece rate is paid equals or exceeds the number of hours worked in excess of the applicable statutory maximum (currently 40 hours) for the particular workweek; and*

- *The compensation paid for the overtime is at least equal to pay at one and one-half times the applicable minimum rate for the total number of hours worked in excess of 40 hours.*

The piece rate is a bona fide rate if it is the rate actually paid for work performed during non-overtime hours and it is sufficient to yield at least the minimum wage per hour. If a piece worker works at two or more kinds of work for different straight time piece rates, and if by agreement the employee is paid at a rate not less than one and one-half times whichever straight time piece rate is applicable to the work performed during the overtime hours, then such a rate must meet all the other conditions discussed above.

Some piece rate employees are also guaranteed a minimum hourly rate. When the employee's total piece rate earnings for the workweek fall short of the amount that would be earned for the hours worked at the guaranteed rate the employee is paid the difference. In this case, the employee is actually paid at an hourly rate and that rate is the regular rate. If an employee works at both hourly and piece rates then the overtime rate due is one and one-half times the hourly or piece rate applicable to the type of work being performed during the overtime hours.

Employees paid a flat sum for a day's work or for doing a particular job, without regard to the number of hours worked in the day or at the job, are paid on a day/task rate basis. When the employee receives no other forms of compensation the regular rate is determined by totaling the sums received (day rates and/or task rates) for the workweek and dividing that total by the total number of hours actually worked. The employee is entitled to extra half time pay for all the hours worked over 40 in the workweek.

When an employee is paid on a task rate basis, without regard to the actual number of hours it takes to complete the job, overtime pay issues may arise because the wrong rate may be applied or the employee may not be paid for all hours actually worked. For example, it may be determined that an employee (or group) should complete a particular task in eight hours and upon completion of the task the employee is credited with eight hours "worked" even though the actual hours worked may be more or less than eight. At the end of the workweek the employee is paid for the first credited 40 hours and one and one-half times for credited hours over 40. The number of hours credited and paid to the employee bear no necessary relationship to the number of hours actually worked. The employee's regular rate has to be determined by taking the amount paid for the task and dividing it by the actual hours worked, not the credited hours. The employee is entitled to be paid overtime at one and one-half times the determined regular rate for all hours actually worked above 40 in the workweek.

Alternative Pay Plans

Generally, employers must pay overtime in cash wages on the next regular payday for the pay period in which the overtime is worked. However, the FLSA and the Department of Labor recognize some alternative overtime pay plans which some employers may be able to utilize. For all of the alternative pay plans, employers must meet any specific criteria of the plan before utilizing the plan. Each alternative pay plan is discussed below.

Belo Plans

A Belo plan allows an employer to make fixed payments to an employee when the employee's duties necessitate irregular work hours and the total wages would vary from week to week if they were calculated on an hourly rate basis. Belo plans must meet very specific criteria in order to be recognized as valid by the Department of Labor. A Belo plan provides for a set regular rate and for a guaranteed payment.

The employee's duties must necessitate significant variations in the weekly hours of work both above and below the statutory weekly limit on non-overtime hours. A Belo plan is not meant to apply to employees whose varying hours are at the discretion of the employer or employee, nor to a situation where the employee works an irregular number of hours according to a predetermined schedule. It must be the duties which necessitate the irregular hours. Some examples of types of employees whose duties may (not definitely) necessitate irregular work hours include: outside buyers, on-call servicemen, insurance adjusters, newspaper reporters and photographers, prop men, script girls and others engaged in similar work in the motion picture industry, firefighters, troubleshooters, and the like. It is always a question of fact whether the particular duties of an employee do or do not necessitate irregular hours. Additionally, both non-overtime and overtime hours must be irregular, not just overtime hours.

A Belo plan can only be entered into when the employee is aware of and agrees to the method of compensation in advance of performing any work under the plan. There must be a bona fide individual contract or collective bargaining agreement which sets out the Belo plan. While it is recommended that the agreement be reduced to writing, it is not required. In order to be a bona fide agreement, the making of the contract and settlement of its terms must be done in good faith.

A Belo plan must specify a regular rate, it must provide for overtime compensation for all hours worked in excess of the maximum hours standard (40), and it must specify a weekly pay guarantee for not more than 60 hours based on the rate specified. The regular rate of pay specified may not be less than the applicable minimum wage rate and it must be the actual measure of the regular wages which the employee receives. All guaranteed hours in excess of the statutory maximum (40) must be paid at a rate of one and one-half times the specified regular rate. The weekly pay guarantee must be paid in full in all workweeks, however short, in which the employee performs any amount of work for the employer. The amount of guaranteed pay cannot be subject to deductions or prorated in short weeks. The weekly pay guaranteed may not exceed the compensation due at the specified regular rate for the number of hours specified. The Belo plan satisfies the overtime requirements of the Act because it provides for overtime compensation for a predetermined amount of overtime.

A Belo plan can only cover payments for up to 60 hours worked. However, an employee can work beyond 60 hours as long as the employee is paid overtime for all hours beyond 60. Additionally, for a Belo plan that guarantees below 60 hours, the employee would need to be paid additional overtime pay for any hours beyond those covered by the Belo plan. The Belo plan can guarantee below 60 hours per week, but never more. To qualify as a bona fide contract, the number of hours for which pay is guaranteed must bear a reasonable relation to the number of hours the employee may be expected to work. For example, if the plan provides a guarantee of pay for 60 hours to an employee whose duties necessitate irregular work hours which can reasonably be expected to range no higher than 50 hours, then this plan would not qualify as a bona fide Belo plan. Therefore, the parties need to determine, as far as possible, the range of hours the employee is likely to work. The guaranteed hours should be a low enough figure (probably not the maximum hours likely) so that it may be reasonably expected that the rate will be operative in a significant number of workweeks.

An example of a Belo plan would be one in which the regular rate is specified at $8 per hour and the maximum hours set in the plan is 50 hours per week. The employee is guaranteed pay of $440, $8 times 50 hours, plus overtime pay for ten hours ($40). The employee will be paid $440 each week he/she performs any work for the employer. If the employee works over 50 hours in a week then he/she must be paid additional overtime at a rate of $12 per hour.

In order for a Belo plan to be valid the employee cannot be entitled to any additional forms of compensation that the FLSA specifies must be included in the employee's remuneration for calculating the regular rate of pay. These additional forms of compensation include, but are not limited to, nondiscretionary bonuses, commissions, performance awards, and housing payments. If an employee receives any additional forms of compensation that normally would be included in the calculation of the employee's regular rate then the Belo plan is invalid.

Prepayment Plan

The Department of Labor and FLSA regulations have accepted prepayment of overtime as a valid way to comply with the Act's overtime requirements. There is no objection if an employer pays in advance overtime compensation to become due to an employee in an attempt to keep the wages or salary constant from pay period to pay period. Prepayment of overtime can occur when an employer pays employees a sum in excess of what they earn or are entitled to in a particular week or weeks and the sum is considered to be a prepayment of compensation for overtime to be subsequently worked. For example, an employer may choose to pay an employee for 40 hours in a week when that employee only worked 28 hours. The 12 extra hours are considered prepayment for overtime to be worked at a later date. The overtime credits are computed at a rate of time and one-half, so the 12 extra hours of pay would cover eight hours of overtime. A valid prepayment plan allows for the overtime credits to be used over an extended period of time; they do not need to be used during the pay period in which they are earned.

The employer and employee must agree to the prepayment of overtime credits. Additionally, if an employee works more overtime then has been advanced, the employee must be paid for the additional overtime. At no time may the employer owe the employee overtime. Employers using prepayment plans must have a system to maintain a running account for each employee of the amount of overtime credits.

A prepayment plan cannot be applied to an employee paid a salary under an agreement that the employee will receive the salary even when he/she works less than the regular number of hours in some weeks. Prepayment plans also do not apply to employees paid a salary for a fluctuating number of hours worked from week to week. Since the nature of such employees' employment is that they will receive the fixed salary regardless of the number of hours worked, it cannot be said that they are paid in excess of what they earn or to which they are entitled in any week in which they received the fixed salary even though such weeks may have been short weeks. Amounts paid to employees while absent from work for a vacation, holiday, or sick leave, or for other miscellaneous periods of leave may not be considered as prepaid overtime.

A prepayment plan cannot just be a bookkeeping device used by the employer. There must be an actual advance on overtime. If no attempt is made to get the advance back when the employee severs the employment relationship and credits still exist then the plan is seen as simply a bookkeeping device and not actual prepayments. Further, if at the end of the year the employer just wipes out credits then the plan does not appear to be an actual prepayment plan and may be invalidated.

Time Off Plan

A time off plan is a very rare alternative overtime pay plan. A time off plan applies to a pay period with more than one workweek covered. If an employee works overtime during the first week of a two week pay period and is given compensatory time during the second week of the pay period then no overtime need be paid if a valid time off plan is used. The total wages for the pay period should equal what the pay would be if the overtime were paid and the other workweek paid on the basis of actual hours worked. In order for the time off plan to be valid the employee must be given time off at a rate of one and one-half for all hours worked over 40. Additionally, unlike a prepayment plan, the compensatory time must be taken during the same pay period.

A time off plan can only apply to employees paid a fixed wage or salary; it will not work for hourly workers who work variable work hours and receive variable pay. Time off plans cannot apply to employees paid a fixed salary for fluctuating workweeks.

Earning Based Bonuses

When an employer's bonus payments are based on a percentage of the employee's total earnings these bonus payments may be excluded from the regular rate calculation if specific conditions are met. The bonus must be paid as a percentage of the employee's total earnings, including straight time, overtime, commissions, and/or discretionary bonuses. If the bonus is paid as a percentage of the total earnings then the overtime requirements of the Act will be satisfied because the total earnings are increased by the same percentage and, therefore, include proper overtime compensation as an arithmetic fact. The bonus must pay the same percentage on straight time and overtime earnings, unconditionally.

Pseudo "percentage bonuses" are not valid. Employers may express a bonus as a percentage of both the straight time and overtime wages, but, in fact, the bonus is a sham. Sham percentage bonuses are usually separated out from a fixed weekly wage and the percentage decreases in an amount in direct proportion to increases in the number of hours worked in a week in excess of 40. The hourly rate purportedly paid under this scheme is artificially low and the difference between the wages paid at the hourly rate and the fixed weekly compensation is falsely labeled a "percentage bonus." An example of a sham bonus scheme would be where an employer ends up paying the employee $300 per week regardless. The employer says the hourly rate equals $5.62 per hour (ignore the minimum wage requirement for this example) and the overtime rate is $8.43 per hour. During week one the employee works 40 hours and earns $224.80 plus a percentage bonus of 33.45% equal to $75.20, for a total of $300 in week one. During week two the employee works 43 hours and earns $250.09 plus a percentage bonus of 19.96% equal to $49.91, and total earnings of $300 for week two. In this example there is no overtime compensation being paid. The records reveal that the employer is paying $300 per week no matter how many hours are worked. The regular rate is really $300 divided by the number of hours worked in the workweek.

8 And 80 Plans

The FLSA has a special overtime provision available for hospitals and residential care establishments. There is an exemption from the general requirement that overtime be computed on a workweek basis, if specific conditions are met. Residential care establishments include nursing facilities, skilled nursing facilities, residential care facilities, and intermediate care facilities for individuals with disabilities. The Act's provisions permit a 14-day period to be established for the purpose of computing overtime by an agreement or understanding between an employer, engaged in the operation of a hospital or residential care establishment, and any of his employees. The employee must receive overtime pay for hours worked in excess of eight in any workday and in excess of 80 hours in the 14-day period.

The employer and employee must enter into the agreement or understanding prior to work being performed. The agreement does not need to be in writing and it can be made directly with the employee or through an employee representative. If the agreement is not in writing, then a special record concerning it must be kept by the employer. Overtime must be paid for all hours over eight worked in any workday whether or not more than 80 hours are worked in the period. Any payments at the overtime premium rate for daily overtime hours may be credited toward the overtime compensation due for overtime hours in excess of 80 in the period.

The 14-day period can begin any hour of any day of the week and it is 14 consecutive 24-hour periods. The 14-day period should be chosen with the intent to use it permanently or for a substantial period of time. The first workday begins at the same time as the 14-day period begins. Changes from a 14-day period to the workweek and back again in order to take advantage of less onerous overtime pay liabilities with respect to particular work schedules under one system rather than under the other are not permissible.

CHAPTER 5: EXEMPTIONS

In general, the Fair Labor Standards Act requires covered employers to pay non-exempt employees at least the federal minimum wage and overtime pay for any hours worked beyond 40 in one week. However, there are exemptions from the FLSA's minimum wage and overtime requirements. Some exemptions apply to the overtime pay requirement, the minimum wage requirement, or both requirements of the FLSA. In addition, as discussed in Chapters 9 and 10 - Youth Provisions – Non-Agricultural Jobs and Youth Provisions – Agricultural Jobs, some youths are exempt from the child labor provisions.

Subminimum wage earners are discussed in detail in Chapter 2 - Minimum Wage and will not be discussed in this chapter even though they are exempt from the minimum wage requirements of the Act. Employees who perform both exempt and non-exempt duties in the same workweek are normally not exempt in that workweek. The most common exemptions are discussed in detail throughout the chapter, but below are some examples of all kinds of exemptions.

Examples of employees exempt from the overtime requirements of the Act include:

- *Commissioned sales employees of retail or service establishments (if certain conditions are met);*

- *Computer professionals;*

- *Driver's, driver's helpers, loaders, and mechanics;*

- *Salesmen, partsmen, and mechanics employed by automobile dealerships;*

- *Aircraft salespeople;*

- *Airline employees;*

- *Amusement/recreational employees in national parks, forests, or the Wildlife Refuge System;*

- *Boat salespeople;*

- *Buyers of agricultural products;*

- *Country (rural) elevator workers;*

- *Live-in domestic employees;*

- *Farm implement salespeople;*

- *Firefighters in small public fire departments (less than five firefighters);*

- *Forestry employees of small firms (less than nine employees);*

- *Fruit and vegetable transportation employees;*

- *Houseparents in non-profit educational institutions;*

- *Livestock auction workers;*

- *Local delivery drivers and driver's helpers;*

- *Lumber operations employees of small firms (less than nine employees);*

- *Motion picture theater employees;*

- *Police officers working in small (less than five officers) public police departments;*

- *Radio station employees in small markets;*

- *Railroad employees;*

- *Seamen on American vessels;*

- *Sugar processing employees;*

- *Taxicab drivers;*

- *Television station employees in small markets; and*

- *Truck and trailer salespeople.*

Employees who may be exempt from both the minimum wage and overtime requirements of the Act include:

- *Executive, administrative, professional, and outside sales employees;*

- *Farmworkers on small farms (youth workers employed on a small farm with parental consent are also exempt from the child labor provisions);*

- *Certain seasonal and recreational establishment employees;*

- *Casual babysitters;*

- *Companions for the elderly;*

- *Federal criminal investigators;*

- *Fishing employees;*

- *Homeworkers making wreaths (also exempt from child labor rules);*

- *Newspaper delivery people (also exempt from child labor rules);*

- *Newspaper employees of limited circulation newspapers;*

- *Seamen on other than American vessels; and*

- *Switchboard operators.*

White-Collar Exemptions

The executive, administrative, professional, computer professional and outside sales people exemptions from the minimum wage and overtime requirements are called the "white-collar" exemptions. While the exemption criteria for each is unique, they do have some overlapping requirements that must be met. In general, in order for a white-collar exemption to apply, an employee's job duties must meet the criteria for the exemption and the employees must be paid on a salary basis at a salary level of at least $455 per week ($910 bi-weekly or $985.83 semi-monthly). An employee's job title does not determine whether the exemption applies or not; the specific job duties and the employee's salary must meet all the requirements of the Act and its regulations in order for an exemption to apply.

Salary Level

In order for a white-collar exemption to apply, the employee must be paid at least $455 per week as a salary. This requirement does not apply to outside sales people, teachers, and employees practicing law or medicine. An employer may provide additional compensation without losing the employee's exempt status if the arrangement also includes a guarantee of at least the minimum weekly required amount paid on a salary basis. For example, an employee may be paid $455 per week on a salary basis and an additional one percent commission on sales.

Salary Basis

White-collar exempt employees must not only be paid $455 per week, but they must also be paid on a salary basis. Salary basis means an employee regularly receives a predetermined amount of compensation each pay period on a weekly or less frequent basis. The predetermined amount of compensation cannot be reduced because of variations in the quality or quantity of the employee's work. Exempt employees must receive the full salary for any week in which the employee performs any work, regardless of the number of days or hours worked. Exempt employees do not need to be paid for any workweek in which they perform no work. Employers are not required to pay an employee's full salary in his/her initial or terminal weeks of employment or for weeks the exempt employee takes unpaid leave under the Family Medical Leave Act (FMLA).

Exempt computer employees may be paid at least $455 per week on a salary basis or an hourly basis at a rate not less than $27.63 per hour. Exempt employees may also be paid on a fee basis, rather than a salary basis, if the employee and employer agree to payment on this basis. If an employee is paid an agreed sum for a single job regardless of the time required for its completion, the employee is considered paid on a fee basis. A fee payment is generally paid for a unique job, rather than for a series of jobs repeated a number of times and for which identical payments are made. To determine whether the fee payment meets the minimum salary level requirement of the exemption test the employer must consider the time worked on the job and determine whether the payment is at a rate that would amount to at least $455 per week if the employee worked 40 hours. For example, an artist paid $250 for a painting that takes 20 hours to complete meets the minimum salary requirements of the exemption test because the rate would yield $500 if 40 hours were worked.

The compensation requirements of the Act do not apply to certain white-collar exempt employees. Employees engaged as teachers are not required to meet the Act's compensation requirements, and academic administrative employees meet the compensation requirement if they are compensated on a salary basis at a rate at least equal to the entrance salary for teachers at the educational establishment where the employee is employed. The compensation requirements also do not apply to employees who hold a valid license or certificate permitting the practice of law or medicine, or any of their branches, and are actually engaged in such practice, or employees who hold the requisite academic degree for the general practice of medicine and are engaged in an internship or resident program pursuant to the practice of the profession. For medical professions, the exception from the salary (or fee) requirement does not apply to pharmacists, nurses, therapists, technologists, sanitarians, dietitians, social workers, psychologists, psychometrists, or other professions which service the medical profession.

Rules for Salary Basis Payment

If an employer makes deductions from an employee's predetermined salary because of the operating requirements of the business that employee is not paid on a salary basis. An employer may not make deductions when work is not available if the employee is ready, willing, and able to work. There are limited circumstances when an employer may make deductions from an exempt employee's pay and still comply with the salary basis requirement of the exemptions.

Deductions from an exempt employee's pay are permissible when the employee is absent from work for one or more full days for personal reasons other than sickness or disability. If an employee is absent for one and one-half days, the employer is only able to deduct one full day because partial day deductions are prohibited. Additionally, deductions are permissible if they are for absences of one or more full days due to sickness or disability if the deduction is made in accordance with a bona fide plan, policy, or practice of providing compensation for salary lost due to illness (example: a sick day plan). Employers may also make permissible deductions to offset the amounts an employee receives as jury or witness fees, or for military pay. An employer may make deductions from employees' pay for penalties imposed in good faith for infractions of safety rules of major significance and for unpaid disciplinary suspensions of one or more full days imposed in good faith for workplace conduct rules infractions.

Employers may not make deductions from an exempt employee's salary if the employer closes the business for inclement weather or if the employee is absent for jury duty. Additionally, as stated above, no partial day deductions from salary may be made, except during the employee's initial and terminal employment weeks. An employer is allowed to substitute or reduce an exempt employee's accrued leave for time the employee is absent, even if it is less than a full day and even if the employee is directed by the employer to miss work because of lack of work. This type of substitution will not affect the salary basis payment provided the employee still receives payment equal to his/her predetermined salary in any week in which work is performed even if the employee has no leave remaining.

Some employers may seek exempt employee volunteers to take time off due to insufficient work. If an exempt employee volunteers to take the days off for personal reasons, other than sickness or disability, salary deductions may be made for one or more full days of missed work. The employee's decision to take time off must be completely voluntary or the deductions will not be permissible.

Employers who make impermissible deductions from exempt employees' pay may lose the exemption if an actual practice of making improper deductions from employees' salaries is found. The Department of Labor will consider a number of factors when determining whether an employer who made improper deductions should lose the exemption status of certain employees. These factors include the number of improper deductions, particularly as compared to the number of employee infractions warranting deductions; the time period during which the employer made improper deductions; the number and geographical location of both the employees whose salaries were improperly reduced and the managers responsible; and whether the employer has a clearly communicated policy permitting or prohibiting improper deductions. Isolated and inadvertent improper deductions will not result in the loss of the exemption if the employer reimburses the employee for the improper deductions.

Executive Exemption

In order for an employee to meet the criteria of the executive exemption the employee:

- *Must be compensated on a salary basis of at least $455 per week;*

- *Have a primary duty of managing the enterprise or managing a customarily recognized department or subdivision of the enterprise;*

- *Customarily and regularly directs the work of at least two or more full-time employees or their equivalent; and*

- *Have the authority to hire or fire other employees, or the employee's suggestions and recommendations as to the hiring, firing, advancement, promotion, or any other change of status of other employees is given particular weight.*

An employee's primary duty is the principal, main, major or most important duty that the employee performs. The determination of an employee's primary duty is based on all the facts in a particular case, with major emphasis placed on the character of the employee's job as a whole. Customarily and regularly means greater than occasional but less than constant and includes work normally done every workweek but does not include isolated or one-time tasks. These definitions of primary duty and customarily and regularly apply to all of the Act's exemptions.

Managing, for the purposes of the exemption, generally includes, but is not limited to, activities such as interviewing, selecting and training employees; setting and adjusting employee pay rates and hours of work; directing the work of employees; maintaining production or sales records for use in supervision or control; appraising an employee's productivity and efficiency for the purpose of recommending promotions or other changes in status; disciplining employees; determining the techniques to be used; apportioning work among employees; controlling the flow and distribution of materials or merchandise and supplies; providing for the safety and security of employees and property; handling the budget; handling complaints and grievances; and monitoring or implementing legal compliance procedures. The Act's phrase "customarily recognized department or subdivision" is meant to distinguish between a unit with permanent status and function and a simple collection of employees assigned from time to time to a specific job.

The regulations state that the employee must direct the work of two full-time employees or their equivalent, which means the employee may direct the work of one full-time employee and two half-time employees or four half-time employees or any equivalent of two full-time employees and the requirement will still be met. Whether an executive's recommendations as to another employee's status are given particular weight, so as to qualify for the exemption, is determined on a case-by-case basis. Factors which should be considered include whether it is part of the employee's job duties to make recommendations and the frequency of such recommendations, as well as the frequency the recommendations are requested and/or relied upon. Generally, an executive's recommendations must pertain to employees the executive customarily and regularly directs and they cannot be just occasional suggestions. An executive's recommendations may be deemed to have "particular weight" even if a higher level manager's recommendations have more importance, and even if the executive does not have the authority to make the ultimate decision as to the employee's change in status.

An executive who owns at least a bona fide 20% interest in the enterprise in which employed, regardless of the type of organization, and who is actively engaged in its management is considered a bona fide exempt executive.

Administrative Exemption

In order for an employee to meet the criteria for the administrative exemption, the employee:

- *Must be compensated on a salary or fee basis at a rate not less than $455 per week;*

- *Have a primary duty which is the performance of office or non-manual work directly related to the management or general business operations of the employer or the employer's customer; and*

- *The primary duty includes the exercise of independent judgment and discretion with respect to matters of significance.*

In order to meet the "directly related to management or general business operations" requirement, an employee must perform work directly related to helping with the running or servicing of the business, as opposed to duties such as working on a manufacturing production line or selling a product in a retail or service establishment. The type of work which meets the requirement includes, but is not limited to, work in functional areas such as tax, finance, accounting, budgeting, auditing, insurance, quality control, purchasing, advertising, marketing, research, procurement, safety and health, human resources, employee benefits, labor relations, personnel management, government relations, computer network, Internet and database administration, public relations, legal and regulatory compliance and similar activities. Since the primary duty requirement may be met if an employee does work related to the management or general business operations of the employer's customer, an employee who acts as an advisor or consultant to their employer's clients or customers (for example as tax experts or financial consultants) may be exempt.

Generally, the exercise of discretion and independent judgment involves comparing and assessing the possible courses of conduct and making a decision after considering all possibilities. For the Act's purposes, this requirement must be applied while looking at all the facts involved in the employee's particular employment situation, and implies the employee has the authority to make choices free from immediate supervision or direction. Factors to consider in determining whether the employee exercises discretion and independent judgment include whether the employee:

- *Has authority to formulate, affect, interpret, or implement management policies or operating practices;*

- *Performs work that affects business operations to a substantial degree;*

- *Carries out major assignments in conducting the operations of the business;*

- *Has authority to commit the employer in matters that have significant financial impact;*

- *Has the authority to waive or deviate from established policies and procedures without prior approval; and*

- *Any other factors set forth in the Act's regulations.*

If an employee's decisions are revised or reversed after review it does not mean the employee is not exercising discretion and independent judgment. Additionally, the use of independent judgment and discretion must be more than the use of skill in applying well established techniques, procedures, or specific standards described in manuals or other sources.

The requirements for the exemption require that the employee exercise this discretion and independent judgment with respect to "matters of significance," not just any matter. The term refers to the level of importance or consequence of the work performed, and an employee does not exercise discretion and independent judgment with respect to matters of significance merely because the employer will experience financial losses if the employee fails to perform the job properly.

Academic Administrative employees may also be eligible for the exemption if they are compensated on a salary basis at least equal to the starting salary for teachers at the same educational establishment. The employee's primary duty must be administrative functions directly related to academic instruction or training at the educational establishment. Such functions include operations directly in the field of education not jobs related to areas outside the educational field. By its very nature, having a primary duty of performing academic administrative functions directly related to academic instruction or training includes exercising discretion and independent judgment with respect to matters of significance. Educational establishment employees who perform academic administrative functions include the superintendent or other head of the school system and any assistants responsible for the administration of curriculum, quality and methods of instructing, measuring and testing the learning potential of students, establishing and maintaining academic standards, and other aspects of the teaching program. Other employees who engage in academic administrative functions include the principal, any vice-principals responsible for the operation of an elementary or secondary school, department heads in higher education institutions, academic counselors, and other employees with similar responsibilities.

Professional Exemption

There are two types of professional exemptions, the "learned professional" and the "creative professional" exemption. There are also special rules for teachers, and those practicing law or medicine.

Learned Professional

In order to qualify for the learned professional exemption an employee must meet the following criteria:

- *Be paid on a salary basis at least $455 per week;*

- *Have a primary duty performing work requiring advanced knowledge, which is defined as work predominantly intellectual in character and which includes work requiring the consistent exercise of discretion and judgment;*

- *The advanced knowledge must be in a field of science or learning; and*

- *The advanced knowledge must be customarily acquired by a prolonged course of specialized intellectual instruction.*

Professional work is distinguished from work involving routine mental, manual, mechanical or physical work by requiring advanced knowledge. A professional employee generally uses advanced knowledge to analyze, interpret or make deductions from varying facts or circumstances. The Act's regulations hold that advanced knowledge requires education beyond the high school level. The exemption requires that the advanced knowledge be in a field of science or learning. Such fields include law, medicine, theology, accounting, actuarial computation, engineering, architecture, teaching, various types of physical, chemical and biological sciences, pharmacy, and other occupations that have a recognized professional status and are distinguishable from the skilled trades and mechanical occupations where the knowledge could be advanced, but not in a field of science or learning.

This exemption for learned professionals applies only to professions where specialized academic training is a standard prerequisite for entrance into the profession. Having the appropriate academic degree is the best evidence of this requirement being met; however, the word "customarily" means the exemption may also be available to employees in those professions who have the same knowledge level and perform the same work as the employees with a degree, but who attained the advanced knowledge through a combination of work and intellectual instruction. This exemption does not apply to jobs where most employees acquire their skill by experience rather than by advanced specialized intellectual instruction.

Teachers are exempt as professionals if their primary duty is teaching, tutoring, instructing, or lecturing while imparting knowledge, and if they are employed and engaged in this activity as a teacher at an educational establishment. Such teachers include regular academic teachers, kindergarten or preschool teachers, trades teachers, driving instructors, flight instructors, music teachers, and home economics teachers. As discussed earlier, salary and salary basis requirements do not apply to bona fide teachers.

Lawyers and those practicing medicine also meet the professional exemption requirements if the employee holds a valid license or certificate permitting practice and is engaged in such practice. Additionally, an employee holding a degree for the general practice of medicine is exempt if part of an internship or resident program for the profession. Again, the salary and salary basis requirements do not apply to bona fide practitioners of law or medicine.

Creative Professional

The creative professional exemption applies to an employee who meets the following tests:

- *The employee is paid on a salary or fee basis of at least $455 per week; and*

- *The primary duty must be the performance of work requiring invention, imagination, originality, or talent in a recognized field of artistic or creative endeavor.*

The requirement that the primary duty require invention, imagination, originality, or talent distinguishes creative professions from work primarily depending on intelligence, diligence, and accuracy. This exemption depends on the level of invention, imagination, originality, or talent exercised by the employee, and whether the exemption applies is determined on a case-by-case basis. Generally, actors, musicians, soloists, composers, writers, certain painters, essayists, cartoonists, novelists, and others described in the Act's regulations meet the exemptions requirements. Journalists may or may not satisfy the duties requirement for the creative professional exemption. If a journalist's work requires invention, imagination, originality or talent he/she may qualify for the exemption, but the journalist will not meet the requirements if he/she only collects, organizes, and records information that is routine or already public and if they do not contribute a unique interpretation or analysis to the news product. Recognized fields of artistic or creative endeavor include, but are not limited to, music, writing, acting, and the graphic arts.

Highly Compensated Employees

The Fair Labor Standards Act regulations contain a special exemption for certain highly compensated employees. In order to be exempt a highly compensated employee must meet all of the tests for the exemption:

- *Earn a total annual compensation of at least $100,000, including at least $455 per week paid on a salary or fee basis;*

- *The employee's primary duty includes office or non-manual work; and*

- *The employee customarily and regularly performs at least one of the duties of an exempt executive, administrative, or professional employee.*

An example of an exempt highly compensated employee is one who meets the salary requirements and customarily and regularly directs the work of two or more employees even though he/she may not meet the other requirements for the executive exemption. A highly compensated employee's total annual compensation may include commissions, nondiscretionary bonuses, and other nondiscretionary compensation earned during a 52-week period.

Outside Sales Exemption

Another white-collar exemption from the FLSA's overtime and minimum wage requirements is for outside sales employees. In order to qualify for the exemption an employee must meet all the following tests:

- *The employee's primary duty must be making sales (as defined by the Act) or obtaining orders or contracts for services or for the use of facilities for which a consideration will be paid by the client or customer; and*

- *Are customarily and regularly engaged away from the employer's place of business.*

It is important to note, there is no salary requirement for the outside salesperson exemption. The Act defines making sales as "any sale, exchange, contract to sell, consignment for sales, shipment for sale, or other disposition." It includes the transfer of title to tangible property and, in certain cases, of tangible and valuable evidences of intangible property.

Obtaining orders for "the use of facilities" includes selling time on radio or television, soliciting advertising for newspapers and other periodicals, and soliciting freight for railroads and other transportation agencies. "Services" extends the exemption to employees who sell or take orders for services which may be performed for the customer by someone other than the person who takes the order.

To determine whether the sales are away from the employer's place of business one must look at the circumstances surrounding the salesperson's employment. Generally, outside salespeople make sales at the customer's home or customer's place of business. Sales made on the Internet, by phone, or by mail are not outside sales unless they are merely incidental to personal calls. Any set site, whether home or office, used by a salesperson to solicit sales through phone calls or as a headquarters for the work is considered one of the employer's places of business even if the employer is not formally a tenant or owner of the property.

Promotional work may or may not be exempt outside sales work depending on the circumstances under which the work is performed. If promotional work is done in conjunction with and incidental to an employee's own outside sales or solicitation it is exempt promotional work, but promotion work incidental to sales made or to be made by someone else is not exempt outside sales work.

Drivers who deliver and sell products may qualify as exempt outside sales employees if their primary duty is making sales. Numerous factors should be considered to determine a driver's primary duty, including:

- *Comparing the driver's duties with other employees' duties who are engaged as drivers and salespersons;*

- *Determining whether there is or is not customary or contractual arrangements concerning the amounts of products to be delivered;*

- *Whether or not the driver has a selling or solicitor's license when required by law;*

- *How the employee's occupation is described in collective bargaining agreements; and*

- *Any other factors determined by the Department of Labor and the Act's regulations to have bearing on the determination.*

Computer Professional Exemption

Certain computer professionals may be exempt from the overtime and minimum wage requirements of the FLSA. These employees can include computer systems analysts, computer programmers, software engineers and other similarly skilled workers in the computer field. In order to be exempt, the employee must meet all of the criteria for the exemption:

- *The employee must be paid on a salary or fee basis of at least $455 per week or $27.63 per hour;*

- *Be employed as a computer systems analyst, computer programmer, software engineer, or in other similarly skilled fields; and*

- *The employee's primary duty must consist of:*

  - *Applying systems analyst techniques and procedures, including consulting with users, to determine hardware, software or system functional specifications;*

  - *Design, development, documentation, analysis, creation, testing, or modification of computer systems or programs, including prototypes, based on and related to user or system design specifications;*

  - *Design, documentation, testing, creating, or modifying computer programs related to machine operating systems; or*

  - *A combination of the previously mentioned duties, the performance of which requires the same level of skills.*

The computer professional exemption does not apply to employees working in the manufacture or repair of computer hardware and related equipment. Additionally, employees whose work is highly dependent on or facilitated by the use of computers and computer software programs, but who are not primarily engaged in computer systems analysis and programming or other similarly skilled computer related occupations identified in the primary duties test are also not exempt under the computer professional exemption. The types of employees whose work is highly dependent on the use of computers, but who do not qualify for the computer employee exemption include engineers, drafters, and others skilled in computer-aided design software.

Other Exemptions

While the white-collar exemptions are the most commonly used overtime and minimum wage exemptions, there are other commonly used overtime exemptions (minimum wage is still due). Three commonly used exemptions are discussed below. For in-depth information on all the Act's exemptions see the Department of Labor's website or contact your local Agency office.

Commissioned Sales Employees

One common overtime exemption applies to commissioned sales employees of retail or service establishments. There are three conditions that must be met for the exemption to apply:

- *The employee is employed by a retail or service establishment;*

- *The employee's regular rate of pay must exceed one and one-half times the applicable minimum wage for every hour worked in a workweek in which overtime hours are worked; and*

- *More than one-half the employee's total earnings in a representative period must consist of commissions.*

All three conditions must be met or overtime is due for hours worked beyond 40 in any workweek. Retail or service establishments are those where 75% of their annual dollar volume of sales of goods or services (or both) is not for resale and is recognized as retail sales or services in the particular industry. An employer must divide an employee's total earnings by the total hours worked during the pay period to determine whether the employee is paid at least one and one-half times the minimum wage.

The Department of Labor has held that the representative period for determining whether more than one-half the employee's earnings consist of commissions can be as short as one month, but no longer than one year. The employer selects the period used to determine if the commission's requirement is met. Employees paid entirely by commissions or those whose commissions are always greater than their salary or hourly pay meet the requirement. If an employee is not paid this way then the employer must separate the employee's commissions and other compensation paid and, for the condition to be met, the commissions must be greater than the other compensation paid.

Tips paid by customers to employees are never considered commissions and cannot be counted toward the commission requirement. However, hotels, motels and restaurants may levy mandatory service charges on customers that represent a percentage of the amount charged for services. If all or part of the service charges are given to employees those payments may be considered commissions. The exemption also cannot apply to employees employed by a central office of a retail chain enterprise as sales instructors working at the various retail establishments since the central office, and not a retail establishment, employs them.

Employers who fail to keep accurate records of the hours worked each workday and the earnings paid cannot substantiate that all the conditions of the exemption are met. It is important that an employer keep accurate records if he/she intends to seek the commissioned salesperson overtime exemption.

Farmworkers

Employees employed in agriculture, as defined by the FLSA's regulations, are exempt from the overtime provisions of the Act. Agriculture includes "farming in all its branches and among other things includes the cultivation and tillage of the soil; dairying; the production, cultivation, growing, and harvesting of any agricultural or horticultural commodities; the raising of livestock, bees, fur-bearing animals, or poultry; and any practices performed by a farmer on a farm as an incident to or in conjunction with such farming operations, including preparation for market, and delivery to storage, to market or to carriers for transportation to market." Work in agriculture does not include work on a farm that is not incidental to or in conjunction with such farmer's farming operations. It also does not include work performed off a farm if performed by employees employed by someone other than the farmer whose agricultural products are being worked on.

In addition to the exemption from the Act's overtime requirements, some agricultural employees are also exempt from the Act's minimum wage requirements. Any employer who does not use more than 500 man-days of agricultural labor in any calendar quarter of the preceding year is exempt from the minimum wage and overtime requirements for the current year. Agricultural employees are also exempt from the minimum wage and overtime requirements of the Act if:

- *The employer is the employee's immediate family member;*

- *They are principally engaged on the range in the production of livestock; or*

- *They are local harvest laborers who commute daily from their permanent residence and are paid on a piece rate basis in traditionally piece rated occupations and they were engaged in agricultural work less than 13 weeks during the preceding year.*

Seasonal and Recreational Establishments

Employees of certain seasonal and recreational establishments are exempt from overtime and minimum wage requirements of the Fair Labor Standards Act. Employees are exempt from the Act's requirements if employed by an establishment which is an amusement or recreational establishments if (A) it does not operate for more than seven months in any calendar year; or (B) during the preceding calendar year, its average receipts for any six months of such year were not more than 33-1/3% of its average receipts for the other six months of such year.

Whether or not the establishment is operating is a question of fact determined by the Department of Labor. However, if the establishment is only engaging in activities for maintenance of operations or ordering supplies during the off season it is not considered to be operating for purposes of the exemption. The "33 1/3% test" takes the monthly average for the six months when receipts are the smallest for the establishment and compares it against the six months when the receipts are the largest to determine whether or not the test has been met. The Act does not require that the six months be consecutive months.

Chapter 6: Recordkeeping and Posting

General Requirements

Record keeping requirements are generally separated into two basic requirements. First, those for nonexempt employees and, second, for those who are exempt.

For nonexempt employees, the following is required:

- *The employee's full name, as used for Social Security recordkeeping purposes, and on the same record, the employee's identifying payroll or employee number,*

- *Home address, including zip code,*

- *Date of birth, if under 19,*

- *Gender and occupation in which employed (it should be noted that gender is required for compliance under the Equal Pay Act),*

- *Time of day and day of week on which the employee's workweek begins. If the employee is part of a workforce or employed in or by an establishment all of whose workers have a workweek beginning at the same time on the same day, a single notation of the time of the day and beginning day of the workweek for the whole workforce or establishment will suffice,*

- *(6)(i) Regular hourly rate of pay for any workweek in which overtime compensation is earned, (ii) explanation of basis of pay by indicating the monetary amount paid on a per hour, per day, per week, per piece, commission on sales, or other basis, and (iii) the amount and nature of each payment which, in accordance with the Act, is excluded from the "regular rate" (these records may be in the form of vouchers or other payment data),*

- *Hours worked each workday and total hours worked each workweek,*

- *Total daily or weekly straight-time earnings or wages due for hours worked during the workday or workweek, exclusive of premium overtime compensation,*

- *Total premium pay for overtime hours,*

- *Total additions to or deductions from wages paid each pay period including employee wage assignments; also, in individual employee records, the dates, amounts, and nature of the items which make up the total additions and deductions,*

- *Total wages paid each pay period, and*

- *Date of payment and the pay period covered by payment.*

For employees working on fixed schedules, the employer is permitted to maintain records showing the schedule of daily and weekly hours the employee normally works. When the employee adheres to this schedule, the employer can indicate that the hours were, in fact, worked by the employee. In weeks in which more or less than the scheduled hours are worked, the employer must show the exact number of hours worked each day and each week.

For exempt employees; i.e., bona fide executive, administrative and professional employees, and outside sales professionals, the employer is required to maintain:

- *The employee's full name, as used for Social Security recordkeeping purposes, and on the same record, the employee's identifying payroll or employee number,*

- *Home address, including zip code,*

- *Date of birth, if under 19,*

- *Gender and occupation in which employed (it should be noted that gender is required for compliance under the Equal Pay Act),*

- *Time of day and day of week on which the employee's workweek begins. If the employee is part of a workforce or employed in or by an establishment all of whose workers have a workweek beginning at the same time on the same day, a single notation of the time of the day and beginning day of the workweek for the whole workforce or establishment will suffice,*

- *The basis on which wages are paid in sufficient detail to permit calculation for each pay period of the employee's total remuneration for employment including fringe benefits and prerequisites. This may be shown as the dollar amount of earnings per month, per week, per month plus commissions, etc. with appropriate addenda such as "plus hospitalization and insurance plan A," "benefit package B," "two weeks paid vacation," etc.*

Posting Requirement

Covered employers are required to post a notice explaining the coverage of the Act in every facility where employees are employed. The poster can be obtained free of charge on the USDOL's website and includes such items, for example, as the minimum wage, child labor, tip credit, enforcement and additional information, along with contact information for the USDOL.

Preservation of Records

The following records must be preserved for a minimum of three years:

- *From the last date of entry, all payroll or other records containing the required employee information,*

- *All collective bargaining agreements, and any amendments or additions thereto; Plans, trusts, and employment contracts; and where such contracts or agreements are not in writing, a written memorandum summarizing the terms of each such contract or agreement; written agreements or memoranda summarizing the terms of oral agreements or understandings,*

- *Sales and purchase records; and, a record of (a) total dollar volume of sales or business, and (b) total volume of goods purchased or received during such periods (weekly, monthly, quarterly, etc.), in such form as the employer maintains records in the ordinary course of business.*

The following records must be preserved for a minimum of two years:

- *All basic time and earning cards or sheets which are used for the purposes of entering daily starting and stopping time of individual employees, or of separate work forces, or the amounts of work accomplished by individual employees on a daily, weekly, or pay period basis (for example, units produced) when those amounts determine in whole or in part the pay period earnings or wages of those employees,*

- *All wage rate tables or schedules of the employer which provide the piece rates or other rates used in computing straight-time earnings, wages, or salary, or overtime pay computation,*

- *The originals or true copies of all customer orders or invoices received (order, shipping, and billing records), incoming or outgoing shipping or delivery records, as well as all bills of lading and all billings to customers (not including individual sales slips, cash register tapes or the like) which the employer retains or makes in the usual course of business operations,*

- *All records used by the employer in determining the original cost, operating and maintenance cost, and depreciation and interest charges, if such costs and charges are involved in the additions to or deductions from wages paid.*

Availability of Records

The employer's records are to be maintained either at the facility location or at a central office where an employer maintains such records. At all times the records must be available within 72 hours to an authorized representative of the USDOL.

White Collar Exemptions

Generally, the "white collar" exemptions are the overtime exemptions for administrative, executive, professional, or outside sales persons. Employers do not have to keep the same records for these exempt employees as for non-exempt hourly employees. Even though these exempt employees are generally paid on a salary basis each week regardless of the number of hours worked, an employer may still require these employees to track their working time.

The records required to be kept for an employee under the white collar exemptions include:

- *The name, as used for Social Security record keeping purposes, and employee number or identifying symbol if such is used in place of the name on any time, work, or payroll records*

- *A home address;*

- *Date of birth, if under age 19; and*

- *The employee's sex and the occupation in which he/she is employed.*

Additionally, employers are required to keep records containing:

- *The time and day of the week on which the employee's workweek begins;*

- *If the employee is part of a workforce or group where all workers start the workweek at the same time on the same day then a single notation for the whole workforce is sufficient.*

- *The total wages paid each pay period;*

- *The date of payment and the pay period covered by the payment; and*

- *The basis on which the wages are paid in sufficient detail to permit calculations for each pay period of the employee's total remuneration for employment including fringe benefits and prerequisites. The basis on which the wages are paid may be stated as the dollar amount of earnings per month or week or per month plus commissions with appropriate addenda such as "plus hospitalization and insurance plan" or "plus benefit plan A" or "two weeks paid vacation."*

Commissioned Employees

Most commissioned employees are exempt from the overtime requirements of the FLSA. Employers of exempt commissioned employees must keep records containing the following information:

- *The employee's name,*

- *Address,*

- *Date of birth, if under 19;*

- *The employee's sex and occupation;*

- *The time and day of the week when the employee's workweek begins; and*

- *The hours worked each workday and the total hours worked each workweek.*

- *The total additions or deductions from the wages paid each pay period, including employee purchase orders or wage assignments, and the dates, amounts, and nature of the items which make up the total additions and deductions.*

- *The total compensation paid to each employee each paid period showing separately the amount of commissions and the amount of non-commission straight-time earnings.*

Employers of commissioned employees must also indicate on the payroll records each employee who is paid as a commissioned employee. This indication can be done using a symbol, letter or other notation on the records. Further, employers must keep a copy of the agreement or understanding establishing the employee will be paid on a commissioned basis, and if the agreement is not in writing then the employer must keep a memo summarizing the terms of the agreement. The memo must include the basis of compensation, the applicable representative period, the date the agreement was entered into, and how long it remains in effect. These agreements or memos may be individually or collectively drawn up.

In addition to the recordkeeping requirements discussed above, an employer of a non-exempt commissioned employee must also keep records indicating:

- *The regular hourly rate for any weeks in which overtime compensation is due,*

- *The basis of pay by indicating the amount paid on per hour, per day, commission on sales, or other basis, and the amount and nature of each payment which is excluded from the regular rate,*

- *The total daily or weekly straight time earnings for hours worked, excluding overtime compensation, and the total premium pay for overtime hours, and*

- *The total wages paid each pay period.*

8 And 80 Plans

Employees working for hospitals and residential care establishments under a valid 14-day period may be exempt from the Act's requirements that overtime be computed on a workweek basis. These plans are discussed in detail in the Overtime chapter. Employers of an employee working under a valid 8 And 80 plan must keep records of the name, address, date of birth, if under 19, sex, and occupation of each employee. Employers must also keep records indicating the regular hourly rate of pay for any period when overtime compensation is due, the basis of the pay (per hour, per day, or other basis), and the amount and nature of any payments excluded from the regular rate.

Employers must keep track of the time and day of the week when the employee's 14-day work period begins, the hours worked each workday, and the total number of hours worked each 14-day work period. Further, records must be kept indicating the total straight time earnings paid for hours worked during the 14-day period and the total overtime excess compensation paid for hours worked in excess of eight in a workday or 80 in the work period. The total wages paid each pay period, date of the payment, and the pay period covered by the payment must be recorded. Also, records must be kept of the amount of total additions to or deductions from the wages paid each pay period, and the dates, amounts, and nature of the items which make up the total additions and deductions.

Employers must also keep copies of the agreement or understanding with respect to utilizing the 14-day period for overtime computations. If the agreement is not in writing then the employer must keep a memo summarizing the terms of the agreement and showing the date it was entered into and how long it remains in effect.

Belo Plans

Employers who have set up valid Belo contracts with their employees must keep certain records pertaining to those contracts. An employer must keep all of the records generally required to be kept for non-exempt employees (discussed above in the "General Requirements" section), except an employer does not have to keep records of the total daily or weekly straight time earnings or total premium pay for overtime hours. Instead, employers must keep track of the total weekly guaranteed earnings under the Belo contract and the total weekly compensation in excess of the guaranty. Further, employers must keep copies of the bona fide individual contract or the agreement made as a result of collective bargaining by the employees' representative. If the agreement is not in writing then the employer must keep a memo summarizing its terms.

Piece Rate and Multiple Hourly Rates

The recordkeeping requirements for employees working at piece rates and multiple hourly rates are very similar to those for non-exempt employees working at one hourly rate. Employers must keep all the records discussed above in the "General Requirements" section found at the beginning of this chapter. Additionally, employers must keep records of each hourly rate or piece rate at which the employee is employed, the basis on which the wages are paid and the nature of each payment which may be excluded from the regular rate. Further, the number of overtime hours worked at each hourly rate or the number of units of work performed in the workweek at each applicable piece rate during overtime hours must be kept, along with the total weekly overtime compensation at each applicable rate. The date of the agreement or understanding between the employer and the employee to use this method of compensation and the period covered by the agreement must also be recorded. If all of the workers in the workforce have agreed to use this method of compensation then one single notation of the agreement's date and the period covered is sufficient for all employees.

Noncash Compensation

Employers who make deductions from employees' wages for board, lodging, or other facilities must keep all the records otherwise required, and in addition, records substantiating the costs of furnishing each class of facility. Separate records indicating the cost of each item furnished to the employees are not needed. Instead, the requirements of the Act may be met by keeping combined records of the costs incurred in furnishing each class of facility, such as housing, fuel, or merchandise furnished through a company store or commissary. An employer who furnishes housing to employees does not need to keep separate cost records for each house and can show the cost of maintenance, utilities, and repairs for all houses together. Further, the original cost and depreciation records may be kept for houses acquired at the same time and the cost of furnishing similar or closely related facilities may be shown in combined records.

When records are kept for a "class" of facility, rather than each individual article furnished to employees, the records must also show the gross income derived from each such class of facility (e.g. gross rentals, total sales through the commissary, total receipts from fuel sales). Records must also include itemized accounts showing the nature and amount of any expenditures that enter into the computation of the reasonable cost, and any data required to compute the amount of depreciation of any assets allocable to the furnishing of facilities. The Act does not require any particular degree of itemization but the amount of detail shown should be consistent with good accounting practices and sufficient to enable the Wage and Hour Division Administrator to verify the nature and amount of the expenditures by reference to the basic records.

During weeks when additions to or deductions from the wages affect the total cash wages due in any workweek as to result in the employee receiving less in cash then the minimum hourly wage or the employee works overtime then the employer must maintain records on a workweek basis showing those additions to or deductions from the wages. These records are not required in any workweek an employee is not subject to the Act's overtime provisions and receives not less than the statutory minimum wage in cash for all hours worked.

Tipped Employees

Employers of tipped employees must meet all of the general recordkeeping requirements of the Act and keep additional records. Each tipped employee's pay records must have a symbol, letter, or notation identifying the employee as one whose wage is determined in part by tips. The employer must keep records of the weekly or monthly amount of tips received as reported by the employee to the employer. In addition, the employer must keep track of the amount by which the wages of each tipped employee have been deemed to be increased by the tips, and the amount per hour which the employer takes as a tip credit shall be reported to the employee in writing each time it is changed from the amount per hour taken in the preceding week.

The employer must keep track of the hours worked each workday in tipped occupations and the total daily or weekly straight time earnings for such hours. If the employee also works in an occupation in which the employee does not receive tips the employer must keep records of the number of hours worked on each workday and the total daily or weekly straight time payment made by the employer for such hours.

Subminimum Wage Earners

Employers of subminimum wage earners must comply with all the general recordkeeping requirements of the Act. The Act authorizes the payment of below the minimum wage for certain workers employed under special certificates; these workers include student learners, apprentices, full time students, and disabled workers. In addition to the general recordkeeping requirements employers must segregate on the payroll or pay records the names and required information with respect to those employees employed under special certificates. A symbol, letter, or notation may be placed before each name indicating the person is a learner, apprentice, student, or handicapped worker. The employer must also keep copies of the certificate under which the employee is employed.

Homeworkers

For industrial homeworkers, employers must comply with the FLSA's general recordkeeping requirements and keep additional records required for all homeworkers.

With respect to each lot of work given to the employee, the employer must keep records including:

- *The date on which work is given out to the worker or is begun by the worker, and the amount of such work given or begun;*

- *The date the work is turned in and the amount of work turned in;*

- *The kind of articles worked on and the operations performed;*

- *The piece rates paid;*

- *The hours worked on each lot turned in; and*

- *The wages paid for each lot of work turned in.*

With respect to any agent, distributor, or contractor the employer uses, the employer must keep track of the name and address of each such agent, distributor, or contractor through whom homework is distributed or collected, and the name and address of each homeworker whom work is distributed to or collected from.

In addition to the above records, employers of industrial homeworkers must keep a Homeworker Handbook (the "Handbook") for each homeworker. A Handbook may be obtained from the Wage and Hour Division. The employer gives the Handbook to the worker in order to insure that the hours worked and other required information is entered by the homeworker when work is performed and/or business related expenses are incurred. The homeworker must remain in possession of the Handbook except at the end of each pay period when it is to be submitted to the employer for transcription of hours worked and other information required to compute the wages to be paid.

All Handbooks should include a provision for written verification by the employer attesting that the homeworker was instructed to accurately record all of the required information regarding such homeworker's employment and that, to the best of the employer's knowledge or belief, the information was recorded accurately. Once a Handbook is full, or upon termination of employment, the Handbook is to be returned to the employer. Employers must preserve and maintain handbooks for at least two years and make them available for inspection by the Wage and Hour Division upon request.

Time Clocks and Rounding

Time clocks are not required by the FLSA, but they are not prohibited from use. When a time clock is used, if an employee voluntarily comes in to work before his/her regular start time or remains after quitting time then the employee does not have to be paid for such period provided the employee does not do any work during this time. Early or late punching of the clock is not hours worked when no work is done. Further, minor differences between clock records and actual hours worked cannot ordinarily be avoided since all employees cannot clock in and out at precisely the same time. Major discrepancies are not encouraged since that would raise doubt as to the accuracy of the record of actual hours worked.

Some industries using time clocks have a practice of rounding time by recording an employee's start and stop time to the nearest five minutes, one-tenth, or one-quarter of an hour. The Department of Labor presumes these arrangements average out so that all of the time actually worked by the employee is properly counted and the employee is fully compensated for all the time actually worked. Such practices are acceptable, under the Act, for recording working time provided they do not result, over a period of time, in failure to count as hours worked all the time the employees have actually worked (i.e. always rounding down).

Chapter 7: Enforcement
And Penalties

Enforcement

The Department of Labor's Wage and Hour Division (WHD) and the U.S. Office of Personnel Management enforce the Fair Labor Standards Act. The WHD enforces the Act for employees of private business, state and local governments, and federal employees of the Library of Congress, United States Postal Service, Postal Rate Commission, and the Tennessee Valley Authority. The Office of Personnel Management enforces the FLSA for other Federal employees and the U.S. Congress for congressional employees.

Wage and Hour Division investigators conduct investigations and gather data on wages, hours worked, and other employment conditions or practices, in order to determine whether the law is complied with properly. Investigators are stationed at local WHD offices throughout the United States. Investigators who discover violations may recommend changes in the employer's practices to bring the employer into compliance. It is a violation, under the law, to fire or in any other way discriminate against an employee for filing a complaint under the Act or for participating in a legal proceeding or investigation.

Investigations

Investigations by the WHD are often initiated by a complaint filed with the Division. All complaints are generally kept confidential; the name of the complainant and the nature of the complaint are not disclosed. A complainant's identity is only disclosed when it is necessary to pursue an allegation and the complainant has given permission to disclose his/her identity. In addition to investigations initiated by complaints, the WHD also sometimes selects certain types of businesses or industries for investigations without complaints filed. Occasionally, a number of businesses in a certain industry or geographical area are examined by the WHD for FLSA compliance. In either situation, the WHD's objective is to ensure compliance with the law, and whatever the reason for the investigation, it is conducted in accordance with established policies and procedures.

The following are the steps taken in WHD investigations:

- *A conference between the Wage and Hour representative and representatives of the business is held during which the Wage and Hour representative explains the process to the employer and/or his representatives.*

- *Next, there is an examination of the business's records to determine what laws or exemptions apply to the business and its employees. The records reviewed include those showing the annual dollar volume of the business, the manufacture, handling or selling of goods moved in interstate commerce, and work on government contracts. Any information discovered in the employer's records is not revealed to any unauthorized people.*

- *There is then an examination of the employer's time and payroll records. Wage and Hour investigators take notes, make transcriptions, or photocopy information essential to the investigation.*

- *The Wage and Hour Division conducts private interviews with certain employees. The purpose of the interviews is to verify the time and payroll records, identify a worker's duties in sufficient detail to determine what exemptions apply, if any, and to determine if young workers are legally employed. Interviews are usually conducted on the employer's premises, but other arrangements may be made. In some instances employees, present and former, may be interviewed at their homes, by phone, or by a mail interview form.*

- *When all fact-finding steps are completed the employer and/or the employer's representatives will be told whether any violations of the Act have occurred, and how to correct them. If back wages are owed the employer will be asked to pay the back wages, and the employer may be asked to compute the amounts due.*

Recovering Back Wages

There are various methods the FLSA provides for recovering unpaid minimum and/or overtime wages. The WHD may supervise the payment of back wages, the Secretary of Labor may bring suit for back wages and an equal amount as liquidated damages, or the Secretary of Labor may obtain an injunction to restrain any person from violating the FLSA, including unlawfully withholding the proper minimum wage and overtime pay. Additionally, an employee may file a private suit for back pay, an equal amount as liquidated damages, and attorney's fees and court costs. A single employee may file suit or employees may, together, file a collective action when the employer's violations affect numerous employees. An employee may not file a suit if he/she has already been paid back wages under the WHD's supervision, or if the Secretary of Labor has already filed suit to recover the wages. There is a two-year statute of limitation to recover back pay, except in the case of a willful violation by the employer then the statute of limitations is three years.

Penalties

There are various penalties employers may face if they violate the Act. Employers who willfully or repeatedly violate the minimum wage and overtime pay requirements are subject to a civil money penalty of up to $1,000 for each such violation. Employers who violate the child labor provisions are subject to a civil money penalty of up to $11,000 for each young worker employed in violation of the Act. Willful violations of the Act may also result in criminal prosecution and the violator may be fined up to $11,000. A second criminal conviction may result in imprisonment for up to six months.

There is also a "hot goods" provision of the FLSA which prohibits the shipment, offer for shipment, or sale in interstate commerce of any goods produced in violation of the minimum wage, overtime pay, child labor provisions, or special minimum wage provisions of the Act. If an employer will not voluntarily correct the violations, the Wage and Hour Division may seek to restrain the shipment of the employer's goods. In addition to the other penalties discussed, the Department of Labor regularly issues news releases regarding egregious violations of the child labor laws.

CHAPTER 8: SPECIAL ISSUES

There are numerous "special" issues or occupations discussed in the Fair Labor Standards Act's regulations. This chapter focuses on just a few of the special issues and occupations covered by the Act. Contact the Department of Labor for information on the special situations not discussed, and for more information on the topics discussed in this chapter.

Financial Service Industry

Financial service industry employees may qualify for the administrative exemption under the Act. To review, in order to qualify for the administrative employee exemption an employee must:

- *Be compensated on a salary or fee basis at a rate not less than $455 per week;*

- *The employee's primary duty is the performance of office or non-manual work directly related to the management or general business operations of the employer or the employer's customers; and*

- *The primary duty includes the exercise of discretion and independent judgment with regard to matters of significance.*

Employees in the financial service industry generally meet the primary duty requirement of the administrative exemption if their duties include work collecting and analyzing information regarding a customer's income, assets, investments or debts; the employees determine which financial products best meet the customer's needs and financial circumstances; the employees advise the customer of the advantages and disadvantages of different financial products; and employees market, service or promote the employer's financial products. Whether an employee's activities are aimed at an end user or an intermediary does not matter for purposes of determining whether the exemption applies. Employees who perform these types of duties in the financial service industry will generally meet the administrative exemption requirement of the Fair Labor Standards Act. However, an employee whose primary duty is just to sell financial products does not qualify for the administrative exemption.

Insurance Claims Adjusters

Insurance claims adjusters may qualify for the FLSA's administrative exemption from overtime and minimum wage pay requirements. Generally, whether an insurance claims adjuster works for an insurance company or other type of company the adjuster meets the duties requirement of the administrative exemption if his/her duties include such activities as:

- *Interviewing the insured, witnesses, and physicians;*

- *Inspecting property damage;*

- *Reviewing factual information to prepare damage estimates;*

- *Evaluating and making recommendations regarding coverage of claims;*

- *Determining liability and total value of a claim;*

- *Negotiating settlements; and*

- *Making recommendations regarding litigation.*

Whether the employee meets the exemption's requirements does not depend solely on the employee's title as a "claims adjuster." Determining whether the exemption applies must be made using a case-by-case assessment of each employee's duties.

Security Guard and Maintenance Service Industries

Employers may have questions regarding whether the FLSA applies to employees in the security guard or maintenance service industries. The security guard service industry includes firms that provide protection to firms or individuals. Security guards normally obtain a state license that is portable from firm to firm, and guards cover a post daily and are usually paid on an hourly basis. The maintenance service industry includes firms that generally provide janitorial services, and provide the materials necessary to do the cleaning. Maintenance service employees generally perform work at one or more locations during each work shift. Employers in these industries usually must provide their workers with minimum wage, overtime pay, and keep records according to the Act's requirements. Only those employees who meet an FLSA exemption do not have to be paid minimum wage and/or overtime; however, in general both security guards and maintenance service industry workers are non-exempt.

Security guards cannot be required to bear the cost of their uniform, gun, whistle, belt or other employer or industry required tools if by purchasing these items the employees receive less than minimum wage per hour, or the cost of the items cut into any overtime wages earned. This applies whether the employee buys the uniform or tools directly or the employer sells the items to employees. Additionally, security guards cannot be required to bear the cost of dry cleaning their uniforms if doing so would result in the employees receiving less than minimum wage or the cost cuts into any overtime pay earned.

Security guards must be paid overtime on a workweek basis; their hours cannot be averaged over a two-week period. Further, hours worked by a guard in more than one post during the same workweek must be counted together for overtime purposes, and travel between work posts (sites) must also be treated as hours worked. All hours worked must be recorded. The Department of Labor has found that some security guard firms try to hide hours worked by showing "expense" payments to guards for hours worked over 40 in one workweek; this practice is illegal.

Fair Labor Standards Act issues also arise in the maintenance service industry where some firms do not pay all workers. Every person who works must receive payment, so if a husband and wife team or other family members work together, each member of the family must be on the payroll and receive the proper compensation for their hours worked. Any employees who are under age 16 cannot be permitted to work past 7:00 pm (9:00 pm from June 1 – Labor Day), and all minors who work for these firms must receive the proper compensation. Non-exempt maintenance service industry employees must be paid overtime for all hours worked above 40 in a workweek, regardless of the method of compensation. Hours worked by a janitor in more than one establishment during the same workweek must be counted together for overtime purposes.

Interns and Volunteers

Many employers have questions regarding whether or not internships and volunteer opportunities are allowed under the FLSA. Determining whether an individual may volunteer or intern at an organization under the Act depends on the circumstances of each case. In general, if an internship or volunteer program does not meet the FLSA's regulation requirements then the individuals in those programs are seen as employees and must be paid minimum wage and overtime as required by the Act.

Internship and Training Programs

Internships and training programs in the "for-profit," private sector are most often viewed as employment unless a specific test related to trainees is met. Interns who qualify as employees rather than trainees typically must be paid at least minimum wage and overtime pay.

There are certain circumstances when training or internship participants do not need to be compensated at for-profit, private sector jobs. The Supreme Court has held that the term "suffer or permit to work," used to describe employment under the Act, cannot be interpreted so as to make a person whose work serves only his/her own interest an employee of another who provides aide or instruction. Training interns for their own educational benefits must meet certain criteria to be excluded from the definition of employment and each program is evaluated based on all the facts and circumstances of that situation.

There are six criteria which must be met for an internship or training program to be excluded from employment under the Act.

- *The internship is similar to training which would be given in an educational environment even though it includes actual operation of the employer's facilities.*

- *The internship is for the benefit of the intern.*

- *The intern does not displace regular employees, but works under the close supervision of existing staff.*

- *The employer that provides the training derives no immediate advantage from the activities of the interns, and, on occasion, the internship program may actually impede the employer's operations.*

- *The intern is not necessarily entitled to a job at the conclusion of the internship.*

- *The employer and the intern understand that the intern is not entitled to wages for the time spent in the internship.*

If all of the factors above are met, an employment relationship does not exist under the FLSA and the Act's minimum wage and overtime pay requirements do not apply to the intern. This is to be viewed as a very narrow exclusion from the definition of employment.

The more an internship program is structured around a classroom or academic experience, as opposed to the employer's actual operations, the more likely the internship will be viewed as an extension of the individual's education experience (criteria number one described above). This often occurs where a college or university exercises oversight over the internship program and provides education credit. Additionally, the more the program provides the individual with skills that can be used in multiple employment settings, as opposed to skills particular to that one employer's operations, the more likely the intern will be viewed as receiving training.

The business cannot be dependent on the work of the intern and the intern should not be performing routine work of the business on a regular and/or recurring basis. If interns are engaged in the operations of the employer or are performing productive work (i.e., filing, other clerical work, or assisting customers) then the fact that the interns may be receiving some benefits in the form of new skills or improved work habits will not exclude them from the FLSA's minimum wage and overtime requirements because the employer benefits from the interns' work.

An employer who uses interns as substitutes for regular workers or to augment the existing workforce during specific periods has to pay those interns minimum wage and overtime pay. If the employer would have hired extra staff or required existing staff to work longer hours if not for the interns, then the interns are viewed as employees and are entitled to compensation. However, if the employer is providing job-shadowing opportunities that allow an intern to learn certain functions under close and constant supervision of regular employees but the interns perform little to no work, the activity is more likely to be viewed as a bona fide educational experience. If interns receive the same level of supervision as the employer's regular workers, this would suggest an employment relationship rather than a training relationship.

Internships should be of a fixed duration, established prior to the beginning of the internship. Employers should not use unpaid internships as trial periods for individuals seeking employment at the conclusion of the internship period. If an intern is placed with the employer for a trial period with the expectation that he/she will then be hired on a permanent basis, then that individual is generally considered an employee, not an intern.

Public Sector and Non-profit Internships

The Wage and Hour Division of the Department of Labor (WHD) recognizes an exception to the strict internship requirements discussed above for certain individuals who wish to intern or volunteer services in the public sector. There is a special exception for individuals who volunteer to perform services for a state or local government agency and individuals who volunteer for humanitarian purposes for private non-profit food banks. The WHD also recognizes an exception for individuals who volunteer their time freely and without anticipation of compensation for religious, charitable, civic, or humanitarian purposes at non-profit organizations. Unpaid internships in the public sector and at non-profit charitable organizations, where the intern volunteers without expectation of compensation, are generally permissible under the FLSA.

Volunteers

Unpaid volunteers for public service, religious, or humanitarian objectives are not considered employees of the religious, charitable, or similar non-profit organizations that receive their services. Employees may not volunteer services to for-profit, private sector employers, but individuals generally can volunteer services to their public sector employers. However, a public sector employer may not allow their employees to volunteer, without compensation, additional time to do the same work for which they are employed. A public sector employee who chooses to volunteer time, outside of the workday, for his/her employer must volunteer in a capacity other than the job for which he/she is hired. For example, a secretary at a non-profit may choose to volunteer time serving meals in the non-profit's soup kitchen, but he/she cannot volunteer to file or do data entry if those duties are part of her employment duties.

CHAPTER 9: YOUTH PROVISIONS - NON-AGRICULTURAL JOBS

The Youth Labor provisions of the FLSA differ for agricultural and non-agricultural jobs. This chapter focuses on the child labor provisions regarding non-agricultural jobs. It is important to note that many states place tighter restrictions on child labor than the FLSA; an employer should check with his/her State's Department of Labor to verify he/she is in compliance with both federal and state laws. When both federal and state laws are applicable to child labor, the law with the stricter standards must be obeyed.

The FLSA enacted the youth provisions of the Act to ensure that when young people work the job does not jeopardize their health, well-being, or educational opportunities. While the FLSA's youth provisions cover many aspects of employment, the provisions do not:

- *Require minors to obtain "working papers" or work permits;*

- *Restrict the number of hours or times of day that workers 16 years of age and older may be employed;*

- *Apply where no FLSA employment relationship exists;*

- *Regulate or require such things as breaks, meal periods, or fringe benefits; or*

- *Regulate such issues as discrimination harassment, verbal or physical abuse, or morality.*

Other Federal or State laws may govern the above issues, but the FLSA does not.

The Federal child labor provisions do not apply to some minor workers. The provisions do not apply to:

- *Children 16 and 17 years of age employed by their parents in occupations other than those declared hazardous by the Secretary of Labor;*

- *Children under 16 employed by their parents in occupations other than mining or manufacturing, or occupations declared hazardous by the Secretary of Labor;*

- *Children employed as actors or performers in motion pictures, theatrical, radio, or television productions;*

- *Children engaged in the delivery of newspapers to the consumer; and*

- *Homeworkers engaged in the making of wreaths composed principally of natural holly, pine, cedar, or other evergreens (including the harvesting of the evergreens).*

Hours and Standards

The FLSA's youth provisions for non-agricultural jobs establish both hours and occupational standards for minors. Once a youth reaches age 18, he/she is no longer subject to the child labor provisions of the Act. Generally, children of any age are permitted to work for businesses entirely owned by their parents, except youths under 16 years old may not be employed in mining or manufacturing and no one under the age of 18 may be employed in any occupation the Secretary of Labor has deemed hazardous.

Age 16 is the basic minimum age for most unrestricted employment. Sixteen- and 17-year-olds may be employed for unlimited hours in any occupation other than those declared hazardous by the Secretary of Labor. Youths 14 and 15 years old may be employed outside school hours in a variety of non-manufacturing, non-hazardous jobs for limited periods of time and under specified conditions. Youths under 14 years of age may not be employed in non-agricultural occupations covered by the FLSA. Permissible employment for such children is limited to work that is exempt from FLSA coverage, such as delivering newspapers to the consumer and acting. Children may also perform work not covered by the FLSA like minor chores around private homes or casual babysitting.

Sixteen- and 17-Year-Olds

Sixteen- and 17-year-old minors are permitted to work in most employment, and they may be employed for unlimited hours on any days. The only jobs which 16- and 17-year-olds cannot be employed in are those occupations which the Secretary of Labor "shall find and by order declare" to be particularly hazardous for persons under the age of 18. This minimum age requirement for those occupations applies even if the minor is employed by his/her parent or a person standing in place of the parent. The Secretary of Labor has issued 17 Hazardous Occupation Orders (HO), numbered by the Department of Labor, and listed below in which any minor below the age of 18 may not be employed.

- *Manufacturing and storing of explosives;*

- *Motor vehicle driving and being an outside helper on a motor vehicle;*

- *Coal mining;*

- *Occupations in forest fire fighting, forest fire prevention, timber tract operations, forestry service, logging and saw mill;*

- **Power driven woodworking machines;*

- *Exposure to radioactive substances;*

- *Power driven hoisting apparatus, including forklifts;*

- **Power driven metal-forming, punching, and shearing machines;*

- *Mining, other than coal mining;*

- **Operating power driven meat processing equipment, including meat slicers and other food slicers, in retail establishments (such as grocery stores, restaurant kitchens and delis) and wholesale establishments and most occupations in meat and poultry slaughtering, packing, processing or rendering;*

- *Power driven bakery machines including vertical dough or batter mixers;*

- **Power driven balers, compactors and paper processing machines;*

- *Manufacturing bricks, tile and kindred products;*

- **Power driven circular saws, band saws, chain saws, guillotine shears, wood chippers, and abrasive cutting discs;*

- *Wrecking, demolition, and ship breaking operations;*

- **Roofing operations and all work on or about a roof; and*

- *Excavation operations.*

* - These HOs provide limited exemptions for 16- and 17-year-olds who are bona fide student learners and apprentices.

There are very specific rules provided by the FLSA's regulations regarding teen driving. Any minors aged 16 or younger may not drive motor vehicles on public roads as part of their jobs, even if they possess a valid state driver's license. Minors 17 years of age may drive cars and small trucks on public roads as part of their jobs only in limited circumstances. All of the following requirements must be met in order for a 17-year-old to drive on the job:

- *The driving must be limited to daylight hours;*

- *The minor holds a state license valid for the type of driving involved in the job performed;*

- *The minor has successfully completed a State approved driver's education course and has no record of any moving violation at the time of hire;*

- *The automobile or truck is equipped with a seat belt for the driver and any passengers, and the employer has instructed the youth that seat belts must be used when driving the vehicle;*

- *The automobile or truck does not exceed 6,000 pounds gross vehicle weight; and*

- *Such driving is only occasional and incidental to the 17-year-old's employment. This means that the youth may spend no more than one-third of the work time in any workday and no more than 20% of the work time in any workweek driving.*

Driving by a 17-year-old may not involve towing vehicles; route deliveries or route sales; transportation for hire of property, goods or passengers; urgent, time-sensitive deliveries (such as pizza deliveries); or transporting more than three passengers including employees of the employer. Additionally, the 17-year-old may not drive beyond a 30-mile radius of his/her place of employment, nor make more than two trips away from the primary place of employment in any single day to deliver the employer's goods to a customer or transport passengers other than employees of the employer.

Fourteen- and 15-Year-Olds

The hours and times of day when youths 14 and 15 years of age may work are limited. They may only work outside of school hours, for no more than three hours on a school day, including Fridays, and no more than eight hours on a non-school day. Fourteen- and 15-year-olds may not work more than 18 hours during a week when school is in session and no more than 40 hours during a week when school is not in session. Further, these youths may only work between the hours of 7:00 am and 7:00 pm, except between June 1 and Labor Day when the evening hours are extended to 9:00 pm.

School hours are determined by the local public school in the area the minor resides even if the minor does not attend public school. School is not considered in session if the 14- or 15-year-old youth has graduated from high school or been excused from compulsory school attendance by the state or other jurisdiction once the minor has completed eighth grade and employment complies with all the requirements of the state's school attendance law. School is also not considered in session if the minor has a child to support and appropriate state officers, pursuant to state law, have waived school attendance requirements for the minor; the minor is subject to an order of a state of federal court prohibiting the minor from attending school; or the minor has been permanently expelled from the local public school he/she would normally attend, unless the youth is required by state or local law, an ordinance, or a court order to attend another school.

The FLSA provides a list of those jobs which 14- and 15-year-olds may hold, and those not permitted (not listed) are prohibited. The Department of Labor also provides guidance about jobs that 14- and 15-year-old minors may not hold and a list of non-exhaustive prohibited jobs can be found at the Department's website. The following is a list of those jobs which 14- and 15-year-olds are permitted to have:

- *Office and clerical work, including operating office machines;*

- *Price marking and tagging by hand or by machine, and assembling orders, packing and shelving;*

- *Bagging and carrying out customer orders;*

- *Intellectual or artistically creative occupations such as teacher, musician, artist, computer programmer, software writer, and performer;*

- *Cashiering, selling, modeling, art work, work in advertising departments, window trimming, and comparative shopping;*

- *Errand and delivery work by foot, bicycle and public transportation, except such youths may not be employed by a public messenger service;*

- *Limited kitchen work involving the preparation of food and beverages. Examples of machines the minors are permitted to use are dishwashers, toasters, popcorn poppers, milk shake blenders, coffee grinders, automatic coffee machines, devices used to maintain the temperature of prepared food, and microwaves used only to warm prepared food and that do not have the capacity to warm above 140 degrees Fahrenheit;*

- *Cleaning vegetables and fruits, and the wrapping, sealing, labeling, weighing, pricing and stocking of items including vegetables, fruits, and meats when performed in areas physically separate from a freezer or meat cooler.*

- *Limited cooking duties including cooking over electric or gas grills that do not involve cooking over an open flame, and cooking with deep fryers that are equipped with and utilize a device that automatically raises the baskets from the hot oil or grease. No cooking is allowed with rotisseries, broilers, pressurized equipment including fryolators, and cooking devices that operated at extremely high temperatures;*

- *Cleaning cooking equipment and surfaces (not otherwise prohibited), and filter, transport and dispose of grease as long as the temperature of the surfaces, containers and grease do not exceed 100 degrees Fahrenheit;*

- *Cleanup work, including the use of vacuum cleaners and floor waxers, and the maintenance of grounds, but not including the use of power driven mowers, cutters, trimmers, edgers or similar equipment;*

- *Loading onto motor vehicles and unloading from motor vehicles of light, non-power driven hand tools and personal protective equipment that the minor will use as part of his/her employment at the work site. Also permitted is the loading onto and unloading of personal items such as a backpack, lunch box, or coat that the minor is permitted to take to the work site. Such light tools include rakes, hand-held clippers, shovels and brooms, but do not include trash, sales kits, promotional items or items for sale, lawn mowers, or other power driven lawn maintenance equipment. Youths are not permitted to load or unload safety equipment such as barriers, cones, or signage; and*

- *Properly certified 15-year-olds may work as lifeguards and swimming instructors at traditional swimming pools and water amusement parks.*

Only 15-year-old youths, not 14-year-olds, may be employed as lifeguards and swim instructors at traditional swimming pools and water amusement parks. In order for the 15-year-old youth to be permitted to work in such employment he/she must be trained and certified by the American Red Cross or a similar certifying organization in aquatics and water safety. Additional training is required to work as a swim instructor. Further, those youths employed as lifeguards may not be attendants or dispatchers at the top of elevated water slides. Only work at traditional swimming pools and water amusement parks is permitted. Working at natural environment swimming facilities like rivers, streams, lakes, reservoirs, wharfs, piers, canals, or oceanside beaches is not permitted under this provision. A youth must be at least 16 years of age to be a lifeguard employed at natural environment facilities.

Under certain conditions youths between the ages of 14 and 18 may be employed inside and outside of establishments where machinery is used to process wood products. This exemption applies only to youths who are exempt from compulsory school attendance beyond the eighth grade by statute or judicial order, and are supervised in the work place by an adult relative or adult member of the same religious sect or division as the minor. A minor meeting these requirements is still prohibited from operating or assisting to operate any power driven woodworking machines including starting and stopping the machines and the feeding of materials. These youths also cannot clean, oil, set-up, adjust or maintain the machines. Youths meeting the requirements of this exemption must be protected from wood particles or other flying debris while in the workplace by a barrier appropriate to the potential hazard or by maintaining a sufficient distance from the machinery in operation. The minor employed in this job is required to use personal protective equipment to prevent exposure to excessive levels of noise and sawdust.

Any 14- or 15-year-old who does work in connection with cars and trucks is confined to the following work: dispensing gas and oil; courtesy service on the premises of a gasoline service station; car cleaning, washing, and polishing by hand; and other occupations permitted, but not involving the use of pits, racks, or lifting apparatus or involving the inflation of any tire mounted on a rim equipped with a removable retaining ring.

Work Experience and Career Exploration Program

The Work Experience and Career Exploration Program (WECEP) is designed to provide a carefully planned work experience and career exploration program for 14- and 15-year-old minors who can benefit from a career-oriented educational program. The program is designed to meet the participants' needs, interests, and abilities in order to help youths become reoriented and motivated toward education and to prepare them for the world of work.

State Departments of Education are granted approval to operate a WECEP for a two-year period. Students in the program may work during school hours for up to three hours on a school day and as many as 23 hours in a school week. The students may also work in some occupations that would otherwise be prohibited under the Act. The program participants are given a variance to work in the otherwise prohibited occupations, but no participants may work in manufacturing, mining, or any of the jobs described by the Department of Labor's Hazardous Occupation Orders (HO).

Work Study Programs

Some provisions of the child labor regulations are varied for 14- and 15-year-old participants in approved, school-administered Work Study Programs (WSP). Participants must be 14 or 15 years old, enrolled in a college preparatory curriculum, and identified by authoritative personnel from the school as being able to benefit from a WSP. Prior to administering the WSP, the school must receive permission from the Wage and Hour Division of the federal Department of Labor.

Employment of participants in WSPs is confined to 18 hours in any week school is in session, a portion of which may be school hours. The number of hours a participant may work during school hours is limited and follows a four-week schedule. During three of the four weeks participants are permitted to work during school hours on only one day per week and for no more than eight hours on that day. During the remaining week participants are permitted to work during school hours on no more than two days and for no more than eight hours on each of those two days. WSP participants are still subject to the time of day and number of hours standards established for other 14- and 15-year-old minors.

Penalties

The penalties for violations of the child labor provisions apply to violations of the rules about both non-agricultural and agricultural jobs. An employer may be liable for civil money penalties of up to $11,000 for each employee who is subject to child labor violations. This penalty may be increased to $50,000 for each violation that causes death or serious injury to a minor and that may be doubled when a violation is found to be repeated or willful.

Additionally, the Department of Labor is authorized by the FLSA to seek injunctions to stop the interstate commerce of goods tainted by "oppressive child labor." These injunctions are called "hot goods" injunctions. Interstate commerce of such hot goods is prohibited by the FLSA. The Department may also use injunctions to compel compliance with child labor provisions. In the case of a willful violation of the child labor provisions, an employer may face criminal sanctions.

CHAPTER 10: YOUTH PROVISIONS - AGRICULTURAL JOBS

The Youth Labor provisions of the FLSA differ for agricultural and nonagricultural jobs. This chapter focuses on the child labor provisions regarding agricultural jobs. It is important to note that many states place tighter restrictions on farm work performed by minors than the FLSA; an employer should check with the State Department of Labor to verify he/she is in compliance with both federal and state laws.

There is a partial exemption to the child labor provisions for agricultural jobs: minors of any age may be employed by their parents at any time in any occupation on a farm owned or operated by the parents. The agricultural child labor provisions of the Act do not require minors to obtain working papers or limit the number of hours or times of day (other than outside school hours) that young farm workers may legally work. School hours are those set by the official calendar of the school district where the minor is living (even if the minor does not attend public school).

The minimum age standards for agricultural jobs will be discussed in detail below, but the general standards provide:

- *Anyone at least 16 years of age may perform any farm job, including agricultural jobs declared hazardous by the Secretary of Labor, at any time including during school hours.*

- *Youths 14 years old and above may be employed outside of school hours in any agricultural occupations, except those declared hazardous by the Secretary of Labor.*

- *Twelve- and 13-year-olds may be employed outside of school hours with written parental consent. They may be employed only on a farm where the youth's parent or guardian is also employed.*

- *Youths under 12 years old may be employed outside of school hours with parental consent on a farm where employees are exempt from the federal minimum wage provisions of the Act.*

- *Local youths aged ten and 11 may hand harvest short-season crops, outside of school hours, for no more than eight weeks between June 1 and October 15 if their employers have obtained special waivers from the Secretary of Labor.*

Agricultural employees are not subject to the overtime provisions of the FLSA, and therefore, youth agricultural employees are not subject to those provisions either. Covered minors must be paid at least the statutory minimum wage for all hours worked unless otherwise exempt or employed under the following conditions:

- *Youths under the age of 18 may be paid $4.25 per hour during the first 90 consecutive calendar days of employment, and certain full-time students, student learners, apprentices, and workers with disabilities may be paid below the minimum wage under specified conditions (see Chapter 2 - Minimum Wage).*

- *Any agricultural employer who does not utilize more than 500 "man days" of agricultural labor in any calendar quarter of the preceding calendar year is exempt from the minimum wage and overtime provisions of the FLSA during the current year. A "man day" equals any day during which an employee performs agricultural work for at least one hour.*

Hazardous Occupation Orders

There are 11 Hazardous Occupation Orders for Agricultural Employment (HO/A). A youth must be at least 16 years old to perform any occupation declared particularly hazardous by the Department of Labor. The following is a list of the HO/As, as numbered by the DOL, which no youth under 16 years old may perform.

- *Operating a tractor over 20 power-take-off (PTO) horsepower, or connecting or disconnecting an implement or any of its parts to or from such a tractor.*

- *Operating or assisting to operate any of the following machines:*

  - *Corn or cotton picker, grain combine, hay mower, forage harvester, hay baler, potato digger, mobile pea viner;*

- Feed grinder, crop dryer, forage blower, auger conveyor, or the unloading mechanism of a non-gravity-type self-unloading wagon or trailer; or

- Power post hole digger, power post driver, or non-walking type rotary tiller.

- Operating or assisting to operate any of the following machines:

  - Trencher or earthmoving equipment;

  - Forklift;

  - Potato combine; or

  - Power-driven circular, band, or chain saw.

- Working on a farm in a yard, pen or stall occupied by a:

  - Bull, boar, or stud horse maintained for breeding purposes; or

  - A sow with suckling pigs or a cow with a newborn calf (with the umbilical cord present).

- Felling, bucking, skidding, loading, or unloading timber with a butt diameter of more than six inches.

- Working from a ladder or scaffold at a height of over 20 feet (painting, repairing, or building structures, pruning trees, picking fruit, etc.).

- Driving a bus, truck or automobile when transporting passengers or riding on a tractor as a passenger or helper.

- Working inside:

  - A fruit, forage or grain storage unit designed to retain an oxygen deficient or toxic atmosphere;

  - An upright silo within two weeks after silage has been added or when a top unloading device is in the operating position;

  - A manure pit; or

  - A horizontal silo while operating a tractor for packing purposes.

- Handling or applying toxic agricultural chemicals (including cleaning or decontaminating equipment, disposal or return of empty containers, or serving as a flagman for aircraft applying such chemicals). Such toxic chemicals are identified by the word "poison" or "warning" or are identified by a "skull and crossbones" on the label.

- *Handling or using a blasting agent, including but not limited to, dynamite, black powder, sensitized ammonium nitrate, blasting caps, and primer cord; or*

- *Transporting, transferring, or applying anhydrous ammonia.*

There are a few limited exceptions to the rules regarding HO/As and youth employment. Student learners in bona fide vocational agricultural programs may participate in occupations listed in HO/A one through six under written agreements provided the student learner is enrolled in a course of study and training in a vocational educational training program in agriculture under a recognized State or local educational authority. Additionally the student learner must be employed under a written agreement providing the following:

- *The work is incidental to the student's training;*

- *The work is intermittent, for short periods of time, and under direct and close supervision of a qualified and experienced person;*

- *Safety instruction is given by the school and correlated by the employer with on-the-job training; and*

- *A schedule is prepared of organized and progressive work processes to be performed on the job.*

The agreement must contain the name of the student learner and be signed by the employer and an authorized person representing the educational authority or school. The employer and the educational authority or school must keep copies of the agreement on file. This limited exemption may be revoked if it is found that reasonable precautions have not been observed for the safety of minors.

4-H Federal Extension Service Training Program

Minors, 14 and 15 years old, who hold certificates of completion of either the tractor operation or machine operation training program under 4-H may work outside school hours in occupations for which they have been trained. Occupations for which these certifications are valid are covered by HO/A numbers one and two described above. Farmers employing youths who have completed these programs must keep a copy of the certificates of completion on file with the minors' records.

Vocational Agriculture Training Program:

A minor 14 or 15 years old who holds a certificate of completion of either the tractor operation or machine operation program of the U.S. Office of Education Vocational Agriculture Training Program may work in occupations for which they have been trained. The occupations covered by these certificates are those found in HO/A number one and two described above. Additionally, employers must keep the certificates of completion on file with the minor's other records.

Age Certificates

An employer may want to protect him/herself from unintentional child labor provision violations. An employer may keep on file employment or age certifications for each minor employed to show the minor is the minimum age for the job. Certificates issued under most state laws are acceptable for the purposes of the FLSA.

Recordkeeping

Employers of minors in agricultural jobs must keep certain records required by the Act. Every employer of a minor under 18 years of age in agriculture must maintain and preserve records containing the following:

- *Minor's name in full;*

- *Place where the minor lives while employed; if the minor's permanent address is elsewhere, then both addresses should be recorded. This is required for minor farm workers, other than those employed by a parent, who are employed on days when school is in session or on any day when employed in an occupation found to be hazardous by the Secretary of Labor;*

- *Date of birth;*

- *Written consent of the minor's parent (or person standing in place of the parent), if written consent is required to employ the minor on a farm.*

Employers may be required by the Act to keep additional records for all employees, not just minors, and those recordkeeping requirements are discussed in detail in the chapter on recordkeeping. Employers who employ minors must meet those additional recordkeeping requirements as well. No records are required to be kept if the minor is employed by his/her parent.

Penalties for Noncompliance

Please see Chapter 9 - Youth Provisions – Nonagricultural Jobs for a discussion of the penalties for noncompliance with the child labor provisions. The penalties for FLSA violations of the youth provisions are the same in agricultural and nonagricultural jobs.

APPENDIX 1 – STATE PAYDAY REQUIREMENTS - EFFECTIVE JANUARY 1, 2013

Alabama

None

Alaska

Semi -monthly

Arizona

Semi-monthly; payday two or more days in a month, not more than 16 days apart.

Arkansas

Semi-monthly

California

Weekly, Bi-weekly and Semi-monthly depending on the occupation.

Colorado

Monthly

Connecticut

Weekly. A longer interval (up to monthly) is permitted if approved by the labor commissioner.

Delaware

Monthly

District of Columbia

Semi-monthly

Florida

None

Georgia

Semi-monthly

Hawaii

Semi-monthly; but employees may choose to be paid on a monthly basis under a special election procedure. The Director of labor and industrial relations also may grant exceptions to the general semi-monthly payday requirement. Payday requirement applies only to private sector employment.

Idaho

Monthly

Illinois

Semi-monthly. Monthly payday requirements for Executive, Administrative, and Professional personnel.

Indiana

Bi-weekly

Iowa

Any predictable and reliable pay schedule is permitted as long as employees get paid at least monthly and no later than 12 days (excluding Sundays and legal holidays) from the end of the period when the wages were earned. This can be waived by written agreement; employees on commission have different requirements.

Kansas

Monthly

Kentucky

Semi-monthly

Louisiana

Bi-weekly

Semi-monthly - Applicable to entities engaged in manufacturing, mining, or boring for oil, employing 10 or more employees, and to every public service corporation. Payment is required once every two weeks or twice during each calendar month.

Maine

Payment due at regular intervals not to exceed 16 days.

Maryland

Bi-weekly

Massachusetts

Weekly

Bi-weekly

Michigan

Weekly, bi-weekly or monthly depending upon the occupation.

Minnesota

Monthly

Employees engaged in transitory employment, i.e. migrant workers, which require an employee to change the employee's place of abode, because the employment is terminated either by the completion of the work or by the discharge or quitting of the employee must be paid within 24 hours.

Mississippi

Bi-weekly or semi-monthly

Applicable to every entity engaged in manufacturing of any kind in the State employing 50 or more employees and employing public labor, and to every public service corporation doing business in the State. Payment is required once every two weeks or twice during each calendar month.

Missouri

Semi-monthly

Montana

Wages must be paid within 10 business days after the wages are due and payable.

Nebraska

Payday designated by employer.

Nevada

Semi-monthly

Monthly payday requirements for Executive, Administrative, and Professional personnel.

New Hampshire

Weekly

New Jersey

Semi-monthly

New Mexico

Semi-monthly

Monthly payday requirements for Executive, Administrative, and Professional personnel.

New York

Weekly payday for manual workers.

Semi-monthly payday upon approval for manual workers and for clerical and other workers.

North Carolina

None specified. Pay periods may be daily, weekly, bi-weekly, semi-monthly or monthly.

North Dakota

Monthly

Ohio

Semi-Monthly

Oklahoma

Semi-monthly

Oregon

Monthly

Pennsylvania

Payday designated by employer.

Rhode Island

Weekly, with the exception of Childcare providers who have the option to be paid every two weeks.

South Carolina

Employers with 5 or more employees are required to give written notice at the time of hiring to all employees advising them of their wages agreed upon, and the time and place of payment along with their expected hours of work. The employer must pay on the normal time and at the place of payment established by the employer.

South Dakota

Monthly

Tennessee

Semi-monthly

Texas

Semi-monthly

Monthly payday for employees exempt from overtime provisions of the Fair Labor Standards Act.

Utah

Payments are to be paid at regular intervals, but in periods no longer than semi-monthly.

Vermont

Weekly

Bi-weekly or semi-monthly: Employers may implement bi-weekly and semi-monthly payday with written notice.

Virginia

Bi-weekly

Semi-monthly

Employees whose weekly wages total more than 150 percent of the average weekly wage of the Commonwealth may be paid monthly, upon agreement of each affected employee.

Washington

Monthly

West Virginia

Bi-weekly

Wisconsin

Monthly

Wyoming

Semi-monthly

APPENDIX 2 – STATE CHILD LABOR LAWS APPLICABLE TO AGRICULTURAL EMPLOYMENT - EFFECTIVE JANUARY 1, 2013

———————————

Minimum Age and Maximum Hour Requirements

State	Minimum age for employment		Certificate required to age:		Maximum daily and weekly hours and days per week for minors under 16 unless other age indicated	
	during school hours	outside school hours	Employment certificate	Age certificate	Daily/Weekly	Days per week
Federal: Fair Labor Standards Act (FSLA) applies to migrants and local residents regardless of farm size or number of man-days of farm labor used on that farm.	16	14, 12 with written parental consent or on farm where parent is employed. Under 12 with written parental consent on farms exempt from Federal minimum wage provisions. Local minors (permanent residents) 10 and 11 years old may be employed outside school hours under prescribed conditions to hand harvest short season crops for no more than 8z weeks between June 1 and October 15 in any calendar year, upon approval by the Secretary of Labor of an employer's application for a waiver from the child labor provisions for such employment. The Secretary of Labor has not issued such waivers.	proof of age not required		No provision	No provision
Alaska	16	14	No provision	18	schoolday or week: 9 for work and school combined /23	6 under 18

State	Minimum age for employment		Certificate required to age:		Maximum daily and weekly hours and days per week for minors under 16 unless other age indicated	
	during school hours	outside school hours	Employment certificate	Age certificate	Daily/Weekly	Days per week
Alabama Agricultural employment is exempted from or is not listed among the covered sectors in the child labor laws. Laws generally exclude minors employed by parents on family farms.	No provision	No provision	No provision		No provision	No provision
Arizona	16	14	proof of age not required		8/40 non school period. Schoolday or week: 3/18	No provision
Arkansas	16	14	16	No provision	8/48 10/54; 16 and 17	6 under 18
California	18, 16 if not required to attend school	12	18	No provision	8/40, only on non-schoolday, 12 and 13 8/40 schoolday/week: 3/18 8/48, 16 and 17 4 schoolday, (8 on a schoolday that precedes a non schoolday) 16 and 17 if required to attend school.	6

| State | Minimum age for employment | | Certificate required to age: | | Maximum daily and weekly hours and days per week for minors under 16 unless other age indicated | |
	during school hours	outside school hours	Employment certificate	Age certificate	Daily/Weekly	Days per week
Colorado	16	12	No provision	18 on request	8/40, under 18. 6 on schoolday under 16. In seasonal employment involving perishable products where paid by piece-work, minors 14 or older may work up to 12 hours in a 24-hour period and up to 30 hours in a 72-hour period (not more than 8 hours a day for more than 10 days in any 30-day period).	No provision
Connecticut (separate agriculture child labor law)	16	14	proof of age or agriculture permit required to age 16.		8/48	6

State	Minimum age for employment		Certificate required to age:		Maximum daily and weekly hours and days per week for minors under 16 unless other age indicated	
	during school hours	outside school hours	Employment certificate	Age certificate	Daily/Weekly	Days per week
Delaware (farm work exempt unless performed in hazardous occupations) With respect to non-hazardous employment, agricultural employment is exempted from or is not listed among the covered sectors in the child labor laws. Laws generally exclude minors employed by parents on family farms.	No provision	No provision	No provision	No provision	No provision	No provision
Florida	No provision	14	No provision	18 (proof of age)	8/40 schoolday or week: 3 when followed by schoolday/15. 8/30 when school is in session, 16 and 17. Minors under 16 can work 8-40 during non-school day or week.	6

| State | Minimum age for employment | | Certificate required to age: | | Maximum daily and weekly hours and days per week for minors under 16 unless other age indicated | |
	during school hours	outside school hours	Employment certificate	Age certificate	Daily/Weekly	Days per week
Georgia Agricultural employment is exempted from or is not listed among the covered sectors in the child labor laws. Laws generally exclude minors employed by parents on family farms.	No provision	No provision	No provision	No provision	No provision	No provision
Hawaii	18, 16 if not legally required to attend school	14, 15 in pineapple harvesting 10 in coffee harvesting	16	18 applies only to 16 and 17	6/30 no more than 5 consecutive days, under 14 in coffee harvest in non-school period. 8/40; schoolday or week: 3/18, 14 and 15. 8/48 in pineapple harvesting from June 1 through the day before Labor Day.	6
Idaho	16	No provision	proof of age not required	No provision	9/54	No provision
Illinois (minimum age only)	12	10	No provision	No provision	No provision	No provision

State	Minimum age for employment		Certificate required to age:		Maximum daily and weekly hours and days per week for minors under 16 unless other age indicated	
	during school hours	outside school hours	Employment certificate	Age certificate	Daily/Weekly	Days per week
Indiana (Exempt except for minimum age or when school is in session)	No provision	12	No provision	No provision	No provision	No provision
Iowa (law exempts part-time work in agriculture (less than 20 hours a week when school is not in session and less than 14 hours a week while school is in session) It covers all migratory labor. Law exempts work in the production of seed, limited to removal of off-type plants, corn tassels and hand-pollinating during June, July and August for children 14 and over.	16	14, 12 migratory labor (younger with permit from Labor Commissioner upon court order)	16	No provision	8/40 Schoolday or week: 4/28	No provision

| State | Minimum age for employment | | Certificate required to age: | | Maximum daily and weekly hours and days per week for minors under 16 unless other age indicated | |
	during school hours	outside school hours	Employment certificate	Age certificate	Daily/Weekly	Days per week
Kansas Agricultural employment is exempted from or is not listed among the covered sectors in the child labor laws. Laws generally exclude minors employed by parents on family farms.	No provision	No provision	No provision	No provision	No provision	No provision
Kentucky Agricultural employment is exempted from or is not listed among the covered sectors in the child labor laws. Laws generally exclude minors employed by parents on family farms.	No provision	No provision	No provision	No provision	No provision	No provision

| State | Minimum age for employment | | Certificate required to age: | | Maximum daily and weekly hours and days per week for minors under 16 unless other age indicated | |
	during school hours	outside school hours	Employment certificate	Age certificate	Daily/Weekly	Days per week
Louisiana Agricultural employment is exempted from or is not listed among the covered sectors in the child labor laws. Laws generally exclude minors employed by parents on family farms.	No provision	No provision	No provision	No provision	No provision	No provision
Maine (exempt if not in direct contact with hazardous machinery or substances)	16 unless excused by superintendent of schools	--- except 14 if in direct contact with hazardous machinery or substances	Exempt unless in direct contact with hazardous machinery or substances	No provision	Exempt	Exempt

State	Minimum age for employment		Certificate required to age:		Maximum daily and weekly hours and days per week for minors under 16 unless other age indicated	
	during school hours	outside school hours	Employment certificate	Age certificate	Daily/Weekly	Days per week
Maryland With respect to non-hazardous employment, agricultural employment is exempted from or is not listed among the covered sectors in the child labor laws. Laws generally exclude minors employed by parents on family farms.	No provision	No provision	No provision	No provision	No provision	No provision
Massachusetts	16	No provision	16	No provision	Schoolday or week: 4/24, under 14 8/48	6
Michigan (exempt except for operations involving detasseling, roguing, hoeing, or similar in production of seed)	16	13	Exempt	No provision	10/48 in non-school/week, (11/62 during a school vacation with parental consent) 16 and 17, 48 combined hours of work and school in schoolweek, under 18	6 under 18
Minnesota	16	12	16 for work during school hours	18	Exempt	No provision

State	Minimum age for employment		Certificate required to age:		Maximum daily and weekly hours and days per week for minors under 16 unless other age indicated	
	during school hours	outside school hours	Employment certificate	Age certificate	Daily/Weekly	Days per week
Missouri	16	14	16 during school term	18 on request	8/40 schoolday: 3	6
Mississippi Agricultural employment is exempted from or is not listed among the covered sectors in the child labor laws. Laws generally exclude minors employed by parents on family farms.	No provision	No provision	No provision	No provision	No provision	No provision
Montana Agricultural employment is exempted from or is not listed among the covered sectors in the child labor laws. Laws generally exclude minors employed by parents on family farms.	No provision	No provision	No provision	No provision	No provision	No provision

State	Minimum age for employment		Certificate required to age:		Maximum daily and weekly hours and days per week for minors under 16 unless other age indicated	
	during school hours	outside school hours	Employment certificate	Age certificate	Daily/Weekly	Days per week
Nebraska Agricultural employment is exempted from or is not listed among the covered sectors in the child labor laws. Laws generally exclude minors employed by parents on family farms.	No provision	No provision	No provision	No provision	No provision	No provision
Nevada (exempt except for minimum age when school in session)	14	No provision	No provision	No provision	No provision	No provision
New Hampshire	18, 16 if not enrolled in school	12	exempt	No provision	8 on non-schoolday/48 during vacation. Schoolday/week: 3/23 if enrolled in school. 30 in schoolweek/48 during vacation, 16 and 17 if enrolled in school.	6; 16 and 17 if enrolled in school

State	Minimum age for employment		Certificate required to age:		Maximum daily and weekly hours and days per week for minors under 16 unless other age indicated	
	during school hours	outside school hours	Employment certificate	Age certificate	Daily/Weekly	Days per week
New Jersey	16	12	16	No provision	10 a day	6
New Mexico	16, 14 hardship cases	No provision	16	18 on request	8/44 (special cases (8/48) under 14	No provision
New York	16	14, 12 hand harvest berries, fruits and vegetables	16	No provision	4 a day, 12 and 13	No provision
North Carolina Agricultural employment is exempted from or is not listed among the covered sectors in the child labor laws. Laws generally exclude minors employed by parents on family farms.	No provision	No provision	No provision	No provision	No provision	No provision
North Dakota	14	No provision	No provision	No provision	Exempt	Exempt
Ohio	16	14	18 if residing in agriculture labor camp	No provision	8/40 schoolday/week: 3/18	No provision

119

State	Minimum age for employment		Certificate required to age:		Maximum daily and weekly hours and days per week for minors under 16 unless other age indicated	
	during school hours	outside school hours	Employment certificate	Age certificate	Daily/Weekly	Days per week
Oklahoma Agricultural employment is exempted from or is not listed among the covered sectors in the child labor laws. Laws generally exclude minors employed by parents on family farms.	No provision	No provision	No provision	No provision	No provision	No provision
Oregon	16	12, 9 picking berries or beans for intrastate use with parental permission	Required only for under 18 employed in connection with power-driven farm machinery	No provision	10/40 (more than 10 hours a day with special permit) schoolday/week: 3/18	6
Pennsylvania (exempt from child labor law. Separate law covers seasonal farm workers).	No provision	seasonal farm worker under 14 not to be required to work	No provision	No provision	Employment prohibited from 7 a.m. to 1 hour after end of schoolday of school district where employed, under 18 whether or not registered in such school district.	No provision

State	Minimum age for employment		Certificate required to age:		Maximum daily and weekly hours and days per week for minors under 16 unless other age indicated	
	during school hours	outside school hours	Employment certificate	Age certificate	Daily/Weekly	Days per week
Rhode Island Agricultural employment is exempted from or is not listed among the covered sectors in the child labor laws. Laws generally exclude minors employed by parents on family farms.	No provision	No provision	No provision		No provision	No provision
South Carolina	16	14, 12 with parental approval	proof of age not required		Exempt	No provision
South Dakota	No provision	No provision	No provision	No provision	8/40 schoolday/ week: 4/20	No provision
Tennessee Agricultural employment is exempted from or is not listed among the covered sectors in the child labor laws. Laws generally exclude minors employed by parents on family farms.	No provision	No provision	No provision	No provision	No provision	No provision

| State | Minimum age for employment | | Certificate required to age: | | Maximum daily and weekly hours and days per week for minors under 16 unless other age indicated | |
	during school hours	outside school hours	Employment certificate	Age certificate	Daily/Weekly	Days per week
Texas Agricultural employment is exempted from or is not listed among the covered sectors in the child labor laws. Laws generally exclude minors employed by parents on family farms.	No provision	No provision	No provision	No provision	No provision	No provision
Utah	16	12, no limit with parental consent	No provision	18 on request	8/40, schoolday: 4 (waived with parental consent)	No provision
Vermont	16, 14 with cert.	No provision	16 during school hours	No provision	8/day and 40/week	6/week
Virginia	16	14, 12 with parental consent	Exempt	16 on request	No provision	No provision

| State | Minimum age for employment | | Certificate required to age: | | Maximum daily and weekly hours and days per week for minors under 16 unless other age indicated | |
	during school hours	outside school hours	Employment certificate	Age certificate	Daily/Weekly	Days per week
Washington	18	14, 12 hand-harvesting or cult. berries, bulbs, cucumbers and spinach during non-school week.	18	No provision	8/40, 12 and 13 during non-schoolweek. 8/40 when school not in session, 14 and 15. 10/50 (60 for wheat, hay and pea harvest) when school not in session; 4/28 when school in session, 16 and 17.	7 in dairy, livestock, hay and irrigation, with one day off every two weeks, under 18
West Virginia With respect to non-hazardous employment, agricultural employment is exempted from or is not listed among the covered sectors in the child labor laws. Laws generally exclude minors employed by parents on family farms.	No provision	No provision	No provision	No provision	No provision	No provision

| State | Minimum age for employment | | Certificate required to age: | | Maximum daily and weekly hours and days per week for minors under 16 unless other age indicated | |
	during school hours	outside school hours	Employment certificate	Age certificate	Daily/Weekly	Days per week
Wisconsin	18	12	Exempt		8/40 schoolday/week: 4 (8 before non-schoolday) /18 (24 school in session less than 5 days) under 16. 5 (8 before non-schoolday) /26 (32 school in session less than 5 days) 16 and 17. Minors 14 through 17 may be employed outside of school hours in excess of permitted weekly hours during peak periods. Time and one-half regular rate of pay must be paid after 50 hours per week.	6 12 and 13

Prohibited Work – Night Work and Hazardous Work

State	Nightwork prohibited for minors under 16 unless other age indicated	Prohibited hazardous occupations (HOs) in agriculture to age:
Federal: Fair Labor Standards Act (FSLA) applies to migrants and local residents regardless of farm size or number of man-days of farm labor used on that farm.	No provision	16. Numerous occupations have been declared hazardous in 11 categories of employment including, among others, operating tractors of over 20 PTO horsepower; operating or assisting to operate corn pickers, grain combines, hay movers, potato diggers, trenchers or earthmoving equipment, or power-driven circular, hand or chain saws; working in a yard, pen or stall occupied by a stud animal or a sow with suckling pigs; working inside a silo or manure pit; handling or applying certain agricultural chemicals; and handling or using a blasting agent such as dynamite or black powder.
Alaska	9 p.m. to 5 a.m.	No specific agriculture HOs. Those of general application under 18 are considered as covering agriculture where applicable (e.g. working with power-driven machinery).
Arizona	9:30 p.m. (11 p.m. before non-schoolday) to 6 a.m.	16 (similar to Federal HOs)
Arkansas	7 p.m. (9 p.m. before non-schoolday) to 6 a.m. 11 p.m. before schoolday to 6 a.m., 16 and 17	No specific agriculture HOs. Those of general application for under 16 are considered as covering agriculture where applicable (e.g. working with unguarded belts and adjustable belts)
California	7 p.m. (9 p.m. June 1 through Labor Day) to 7 a.m. 10 p.m. (12:30 a.m. before non-schoolday) to 5:30 a.m., 16 and 17	16, adopts Federal HOs 12 work prohibited in any agriculture danger zone (areas in or about moving equipment, unprotected chemicals, and unprotected water hazard).
Colorado	9:30 p.m. to 5 a.m. before schoolday	No specific agric. HOs. Those of general application for under 18 are considered as covering agric. where applicable (e.g. work 20 feet above ground, operation of power-driven machinery).

State	Nightwork prohibited for minors under 16 unless other age indicated	Prohibited hazardous occupations (HOs) in agriculture to age:
Connecticut (separate agriculture child labor law)	No provision	No specific agric. HOs. Those of general application for under 18 are considered as covering agric. where applicable (e.g. work on ladders, operation of power-driven machinery).
Delaware (farm work exempt unless performed in hazardous occupations)	No provision	16 (adopts, by reference, the Federal HOs). Law exempts those working with adult supervision.
Florida	7 p.m. before schoolday (9 p.m. during holidays and summer vacations) to 7 a.m. 11 p.m. to 6:30 a.m. before schoolday, 16 and 17.	18, operating or assisting to operate a tractor over 20 PTO horsepower, any trencher or earthmoving equipment, forklift, or any harvesting, planting, or plowing machinery, or any moving machinery. 16, operation of power-driven machinery.
Hawaii	6 p.m. to 6 a.m. during coffee harvest, under 14. 7 p.m. to 7 a.m. (9 p.m. to 6 a.m. during any authorized school break) 14 and 15, 12:30 a.m. to 6 a.m., 15 in pineapple harvest.	16 (several), 15 pineapple harvesters prohibited from being on the harvesting machine or the truck attached to it, 12 prohibited from using any harvesting equipment while engaged in coffee harvesting except holding hooks which are free of any attachments or accessories and baskets or containers used to carry coffee berries. They are not allowed to carry loads in excess of 15 pounds.
Idaho	9 p.m. to 6 a.m.	No provision
Illinois (minimum age only)	No provision	No provision
Indiana (Exempt except for minimum age or when school is in session)	No provision	No provision

State	Nightwork prohibited for minors under 16 unless other age indicated	Prohibited hazardous occupations (HOs) in agriculture to age:
Iowa (law exempts part-time work in agriculture (less than 20 hours a week when school is not in session and less than 14 hours a week while school is in session) It covers all migratory labor)	7:30 p.m. (9 p.m.) June 1 through Labor Day) to 5 a.m. with migratory labor permit	No specific agric. HOs. Those of general application for under 18 and under 16 are considered as covering migrant labor where applicable (e.g. power-driven hoisting apparatus - under 18, power-driven machinery - under 16).
Maine (exempt if not in direct contact with hazardous machinery or substances)	Exempt	- (hazardous machinery or substances mentioned in exemption refers to occupations prohibited under Federal law)
Massachusetts	7 p.m. (9 p.m. July 1 through Labor Day) to 6:30 a.m.	16 operation of saw or cutter on a farm except family farm; stripping, sorting, manufacturing or packing tobacco.
Michigan (exempt except for operations involving detasseling, roguing, hoeing, or similar in production of seed)	9 p.m. to 7 a.m., 10:30 p.m. (11:30 p.m. on Fridays, Saturdays and during school vacation periods) to 6 a.m., 16 and 17 if attending school, 11:30 p.m. to 6 a.m., 16 and 17 if not attending school	No specific agriculture HOs. Those of general application under 18 are considered as covering agriculture where applicable (e.g. working with power-driven machinery).
Minnesota	9 p.m. to 7 a.m.	18 (a few) 16 (several including, by reference, the Federal HOs)
Missouri	7 p.m. (9 p.m.) June 1 through Labor Day) to 7 a.m.	No specific agriculture HOs. Those of general application under 16 are considered as covering agriculture where applicable (e.g. working with power-driven machinery, ladders, toxic or hazardous chemicals).

State	Nightwork prohibited for minors under 16 unless other age indicated	Prohibited hazardous occupations (HOs) in agriculture to age:
Montana	7 p.m. (9 p.m. during periods outside school year (June 1st-Labor Day- depending on local standards)) to 7 a.m.	the following agricultural occupations, unless otherwise exempt or working as a student-learner pursuant to 41-2-109 are prohibited: (a) felling, bucking, skidding, loading, or unloading timber with a butt diameter of more than 9 inches; (b) repairing a building from a ladder or scaffold at a height of more than 20 feet; (c) working inside: • (i) a fruit, forage, or grain storage structure designed to retain an oxygen-deficient or toxic atmosphere; or • (ii) an upright silo within 2 weeks after silage has been added or when a top unloading device is in operating position; (d) handling or using agricultural chemicals classified as poisonous; (e) handling or using a blasting agent, including but not limited to dynamite, black powder, sensitized ammonium nitrate, blasting caps, or primer cord; or (f) transporting, transferring, or applying anhydrous ammonia.
Nevada (exempt except for minimum age when school in session)	No provision	No provision
New Hampshire	9 p.m. to 7 a.m.	16 (adopts, by reference, the Federal HOs)
New Jersey	No provision	18 (a few) 16 (a few)
New Mexico	9 p.m. to 7 a.m., under 14	No specific agriculture HOs. Those of general application under 16 are considered as covering agriculture where applicable (e.g. belted, moving, machinery).

State	Nightwork prohibited for minors under 16 unless other age indicated	Prohibited hazardous occupations (HOs) in agriculture to age:
New York	4 p.m. to 9 a.m. day after Labor Day through June 20. 7 p.m. to 7 a.m. June 21 to Labor Day, 12 and 13.	16, adopts Federal HOs
North Dakota	Exempt	(Law specifies that minors under 16 are not to be prohibited from doing ordinary farm work or from operating farm machinery.)
Ohio	7 p.m. (9 p.m. June 1 - Sept. 1 and during 5 or more schoolday holiday periods) to 7 a.m. 11 p.m. before schoolday to 7 a.m. on schoolday (6 a.m. if not employed after 8 p.m. pervious night), 16 and 17 if required to attend school.	16 (same as Federal HOs)
Oregon	Exempt	18 (16 with Certificate of Training) operating power-driven farm machinery of any kind; riding in or on power-driven farm machinery for the purpose of transporting, sorting, delivering, or otherwise processing farm products. State adopts Federal HOs.
Pennsylvania (exempt from child labor law. Separate law covers seasonal farm workers).	No provision	No provision
South Carolina	Exempt	16 (same as Federal HOs)

State	Nightwork prohibited for minors under 16 unless other age indicated	Prohibited hazardous occupations (HOs) in agriculture to age:
South Dakota	After 10 p.m. before schoolday	No provision
Utah	9:30 p.m. to 5 a.m. before schoolday (waived with parental consent)	With parental consent, no age limit for agriculture work, including operation of power-driven farm machinery. Otherwise, HOs of general application for under 18 are considered as covering agriculture where applicable (e.g. power-driven hoisting apparatus).
Vermont	Exempt	No specific agriculture HOs. Those of general application under 16 are considered as covering agriculture where applicable (e.g. operating a machine having an unguarded belt, adjusting belt- driven equipment, and cleaning machinery).
Virginia	No provision	18 (several) 16 (a few) (Generally the same as Federal HOs) Children 16 may operate, assist in operating, or otherwise perform work involving a truck, excluding a tractor trailer, or farm vehicle. Children 14 may perform work as a helper on a truck or commercial vehicle, while engaged in such work exclusively on a farm.
Washington	9 p.m. to 5 a.m., 12 and 13 when school not in session. 6 p.m. to 7 a.m. (6 a.m. in dairy, livestock and irrigation) 14 and 15 on school day. 9 p.m. to 5 a.m., 14 and 15 on non-school day. 10 p.m. (9 p.m. on consecutive school nights preceding a school day) to 5 a.m., 16 and 17.	18 (some) 16 (same as Federal HOs)
Wisconsin	8 p.m. (9:30 p.m. before non-schoolday) to 5 a.m. 12 and 13. 8 p.m. (11 p.m. before non-schoolday) to 5 a.m. while school is in session, 8 hours of rest are required before the start of work the next day.	16 (same as Federal HOs)

Appendix 3 – Child Entertainment Laws - Effective January 1, 2013

STATE	REGULATES CHILD ENTERTAINMENT	WORK PERMIT	LAW/COMMENT
Alabama	Yes	No	25-8-60-For child actors and performers, no employment or age certificate required for persons under age 18.
Alaska	Yes	Yes	Extensive requirements for theatrical employment. 8 AAC 05.300 requires any child under 18 employed in the entertainment industry to have a work permit. Regulations also establish hours of work, working conditions, and prohibited practices.
Arizona	No	No	Sec. 23-235-Minors employed as stars or performers in motion picture, theatrical, radio or television productions are exempt from the law governing persons under the age of 16 if before the beginning of production, the production company provides the Department of Labor with the name and address of the person, the length, location and hours of employment and any other information required by the Department.
Arkansas	Yes	Yes	11-12-104-A child under 16 employed in the entertainment industry must have a permit and the written consent of a parent or guardian for issuance of the permit; written statement from principal as to academic standing of child;
California	Yes	Yes	Extensive requirements for theatrical employment: The Labor Commissioner issues permits to minors to work in the entertainment industry with required documentation from appropriate school districts as applicable and/or permits permitting employment of minors in the entertainment industry.\n\nSec. 6-1308.7-Work permit to work not more than 5 consecutive days in the entertainment or allied industries; excused from school for up to 5 absences per school year; school districts are to allow pupils to complete all assignments and tests missed during absence.\n\nSec. 6750 Family Code - Courts may require a portion of earnings be set aside for the minor in a trust.
Colorado	No	No	Sec. 8-12-104-Any minor employed as an actor, model or performer is exempt from the law

STATE	REGULATES CHILD ENTERTAINMENT	WORK PERMIT	LAW/COMMENT
Connecticut	Yes	No	Sec. 31-23-Minors under the age of 16 are permitted to work in the theatrical industry with the authorization of the labor commissioner. Must have a certificate of age.
Delaware	Yes	Yes	Sec. 508-Special permit issued by Department of Labor allows child under age 16 to be employed in the entertainment industry for a limited time.
Florida	Yes	Yes	450.132-Employers or agents must make application to the Division and notify the Division showing the date, number of days, location, and date of termination of the work performed by minors in the entertainment industry.
Georgia	Yes	Yes	39-2-18-for minors employed in the entertainment industry a permit is required. The Commissioner of Labor must give written consent.
Hawaii	Yes	Yes	Sec. 12-25-22-Minors under the age of 14 may be permitted to work in theatrical employment with written consent filed with the director by guardian or parent; certificate is kept on file by employer. Sec 12-25-23 establishes limits on daily and nightwork hours.
Idaho	Yes	No	Sec. 44-1305 – prohibits children under the age of 16 from certain entertainment activities.
Illinois	Yes	Yes	Sec. 205/8, 8.1-Minors under the age of 16 appearing in theatrical productions must have a certificate authorized by the superintendent of schools; minors employed in entertainment industry may be employed subject to conditions imposed by DOL.
Indiana	Yes	No	Sec. 20-8.1-4-21.5-No certificate required but there are other conditions: must not be detrimental to welfare of child; provisions must be made for education for children under age 16; minor under age 16 must be accompanied by parent or guardian at rehearsal, appearances, and performances; employment cannot be in cabaret, dance hall, night club, etc.
Iowa	Yes	No	Sec. 92.17 – Children under age 16 may be employed as models, outside of school hours, for up to 3 hours a day between 7 a.m. and 10 p.m., not exceeding 12 hours in a month, with parental permission.

STATE	REGULATES CHILD ENTERTAINMENT	WORK PERMIT	LAW/COMMENT
Kansas	No	No	Sec. 38-614 and 616 - Children employed in the entertainment industry are exempt from child labor requirements, except that infants under one month must have written certification from a licensed physician stating that they are at least 15 days old and that they are physically capable of handling the work. Sec. 38-622 - Rules and regulations may be adopted setting standards for minor children on motion picture sets. Sec.21-3604 - Courts may require a portion of earnings be set aside for the minor in a trust.
Kentucky	No	No	Sec. 339.210 - Children employed in the entertainment industry are exempt from child labor requirements.
Louisiana	Yes	Yes	Sec. 253-Minors under the age of 16 must have permit issued by state DOL to participate in employment in the entertainment industry.
Maine	No	Yes	Sec. 26-773 to 775 - Minors under age 16 working as theatrical or film actors are exempt from the child labor law except that they must have work permits and approval by local superintendent of schools.
Maryland	Yes	Yes	Sec.3-207 (a) - Special permit must be issued by the labor commissioner. The permit must be signed and notarized by parent or guardian and employer.
Massachusetts	Yes	Yes	Chap. 149, Sec. 60 - Minors under the age of 16 may take part on the stage in a theater where not more than 2 performances are given in one day and not more than 8 performances are given in any one week with written permission from the attorney general.
Michigan	Yes	Yes	Work permit from local school district for minors 14-17 or Performing Arts authorization from state Wage and Hour Division for ages 15 days to 17 years. There are restrictions.
Minnesota	Yes	Yes	181A.07. Exemptions-Minors are subject to the child labor law except for the minimum age provisions. The labor Commissioner may issue waivers from the hours limitations.

STATE	REGULATES CHILD ENTERTAINMENT	WORK PERMIT	LAW/COMMENT
Mississippi	No	No	
Missouri	Yes	Yes-for under 16	Sec. 294.022 and 294.030 - Need: proof of age, written parental consent and written statement of employer stating nature and duration of job. Waivers of time and hour restrictions may be issued by the director of the division of labor standards.
Montana	No	No	41-2-104. All minors, regardless of age may be employed as an actor, model or performer
Nebraska	Yes	Yes-special permit for a child	Special permit-issued by Dept. of Labor, to exempt from restrictions any child employed as a performer. Need: written parental consent.
Nevada	No	No	Ch. 392. Casinos or resort hotels employing minors in the entertainment industry for more than 91 school days must, upon request, pay for tutoring or other equivalent educational services. Ch. 609 - Courts may require a portion of earnings be set aside for the minor in a trust.
New Hampshire	No	No	
New Jersey	Yes	Yes-for under 16	Sec. 34:2-21.59 - Need: parental consent, good health, workplace approved by DOL, minor under direct care of adult named in application, not attending public school, receiving approved instruction, and not during summer vacation. Number of performances and hours permitted are specified.

STATE	REGULATES CHILD ENTERTAINMENT	WORK PERMIT	LAW/COMMENT
New Mexico	Yes	Yes	A work permit is required at all times when employing children under the age of sixteen issued only by the school superintendents, school principals, other appropriate school officers or the director of the labor and industrial division. The work must also be certified as not dangerous to the child or prohibited as outlined in the FLSA hazardous list. The maximum number of hours allowed for children under the age of sixteen to work is 18 hours a week during the school week and 40 hours a week in non-school weeks. With respect to employing and protecting child performers in the entertainment industry, including motion pictures, theatrical, radio, and television productions, employers are required to follow educational and safety requirements and they are responsible for obtaining a Pre-Authorization Certificate for any child performing under the age of 18 before the employment begins. The certificate is valid for one year or until the specific project is completed, whichever time period is shorter. The employer must provide a certified teacher for each group of 10 or fewer children and must provide a New Mexico certified trainer or technician at the place of employment at all times when a child performer may be exposed to potentially hazardous conditions. The statutes governing child entertainment within New Mexico can be found at the New Mexico Department of Workforce Solutions – Child Labor Section - 11.1.4.10 – 11.1.4.14.
New York	Yes	Yes-models under 18 need permit from educational authorities/ Performer 16-17 needs employment certificate/ performers under 16 need permit from mayor or chief executive	To obtain certificates and permits need: written parental consent (exceptions for emancipated children), proof of age, and a certificate of physical fitness; separate procedures are in effect for New York City and for the remainder of the State. Sec. 7-7.1 Estates, Powers and Trusts Law - Courts may require a portion of earnings be set aside for the minor in a trust.

STATE	REGULATES CHILD ENTERTAINMENT	WORK PERMIT	LAW/COMMENT
North Carolina	Yes	Yes-for under 18 need Youth Employment Certificate from county social services	To obtain certificate need: proof of age. Sec. 48A-13 - Courts may require a portion of earnings be set aside for the minor in a trust.
North Dakota	Yes	Yes-for under 16 need parental permit and commissioner of labor permit	Permits issued if appearance of such minor will not be detrimental to the minor's morals, health, safety, welfare, or education.
Ohio	No	No-performers need parental consent	Performers must be without remuneration and performance must be given by a church, school, academy; or at a concert or entertainment given solely for charitable purposes or religious institution.
Oklahoma	No	No	Minors who entertain are exempt from all laws because they are considered independent employees with agents.
Oregon	Yes	Yes-employer must register with the Bureau of Labor for jobs of short duration (5 or fewer days)-Babies under 15 days can't work; longer duration-minors 14-17 need work permits/ under 14 need special permit from Bureau of Labor and Industries	To obtain work permits need: parental and minor's signature and social security number and proof of age.

STATE	REGULATES CHILD ENTERTAINMENT	WORK PERMIT	LAW/COMMENT
Pennsylvania	Yes	Yes-Minors 7 to under 18 need special permits from Dept. of Labor and Industry, and can't work where there is alcohol.	To obtain special permits need: application signed by parent and employer, and with the seal of notary. Includes provisions for educational instruction, supervision, health, welfare, and the safeguarding and conservation for the minor of the monies derived from such performances
Rhode Island	No	No	With one exception, the state doesn't regulate such employment because entertainers are not employees on a payroll, but are rather independent employees with agents. Therefore regulation is left up to the localities. The state does not permit minors under the age of 18 to work in commercial adult entertainment establishments.
South Carolina	No	No	71-3105-d-The provisions of this Article do not apply with respect to any employee engaged as an actor or performer in motion pictures; radio or television productions, or theatrical productions.
South Dakota	No	No	60-12-1-The provisions of this section do not apply to children employed as actors or performers in motion pictures, theatrical, radio, or television productions.
Tennessee	No	No	50-5-107-The provisions of this chapter shall not apply to any minor who is a musician or entertainer; Minors under 16 may model. Sec. 50-5-201 - Courts may require a portion of earnings be set aside for the minor in a trust.
Texas	Yes	No	Minors under 14 need to submit application for authorization signed by agency and parent, proof of age and a photograph. 13-5(H)-902 & 904. Contracts limited to no more than 7 years. Courts may require a portion of earnings be set aside for the minor in a trust.
Utah	No	No	

STATE	REGULATES CHILD ENTERTAINMENT	WORK PERMIT	LAW/COMMENT
Vermont	Yes	Yes-Minors under 16 need a certificate from Commissioner of Labor and Industry except for certain work done outside of school hours.	To obtain certificate need: written parental consent, Commissioner of Labor and Industry consent, proof of age and school record. Children employed as actors or performers in motion pictures, theatrical productions, radio, or television, or employed as a baseball bat girl or bat boy may be employed until midnight or after midnight if a parent or guardian and the commissioner of labor have consented in writing.
Virginia	Yes	Yes-work permits for Minors 16 and older for cabaret, clubs, dance studio/ for under 16 for theatrical performance. Musicians need permit also.	Child labor provisions do not apply to children employed as actors or performers in motion pictures, theatrical, radio, or television productions. To obtain permit one needs: A completed employer intention to employ form, a permission to employ form signed by parent and school, and proof of age.
Washington	Yes	Yes-work permit for all minors issued by Dept. of Labor.	Work permits required for all minors employed as actors or performers in film, video, audio, or theatrical productions.
West Virginia	No	No	Minors of any age may be legally employed without a permit or certificate in acting or performing in motion pictures, theatrical, radio or television productions.
Wisconsin	No	No- employment can't be in a roadhouse, cabaret, dance hall, night club, tavern or other similar place.	No work permits needed between 12 and 18 for public entertainment. Nothing contained in ss. 103. 64 to 103. 82 shall be construed as forbidding any minor under 18 to appear for the purpose of singing, playing or performing in any studio, circus, theatrical or musical exhibition, concert or festival, in radio and television broadcasts, or as a live or photographic model.
Wyoming	Yes	No	Minors of any age may perform in radio, TV, movie or theatrical productions. Under 16 can be actors or performers in any concert hall or room where there is no alcohol or malt present. Also under 16 must entertain for charity and in reputable place.

Appendix 4 - Selected State Child Labor Standards Affecting Minors Under 18 In Non-farm Employment - Effective January 1, 2013

State hours limitations on a schoolday and in a schoolweek usually apply only to those enrolled in school. Several states exempt high school graduates from the hours and/or nightwork or other provisions, or have less restrictive provisions for minors participating in various school-work programs. Separate nightwork standards in messenger service and street trades are common, but are not displayed in the table. Some states have exceptions or special conditions for minors engaged in specific employments, such as street trades, recreation and entertainment, and jobs in establishments offering alcoholic beverages for sale.

State or other jurisdiction	Maximum daily and weekly hours and days per week for minors of age:		Nightwork prohibited for minors of age:	
	Under 16	16 and 17	Under 16	16 and 17
Federal (FLSA)	8-40 non-schoolday period Schoolday/week: 3-18. Students of 14 and 15 enrolled in approved Work Experience and Career Exploration programs may work during school hours up to 3 hours on a schoolday and 23 hours in a schoolweek.		7 p.m. (9 p.m. June 1 through Labor Day) to 7 a.m.	
Alabama	8-40-6 Schoolday/week: 3-18		7 p.m. (9 p.m. during summer vacation) to 7 a.m.	10 p.m. before schoolday to 5 a.m., if enrolled in school (to age 19)
Alaska	6-day week Schoolday/week: 9 (Combined hours of work and school) – 23	6-day week	9 p.m. to 5 a.m.	
Arizona	8-40 Schoolday/week: 3-18		9:30 p.m. (11 p.m. before non-schoolday) to 6 a.m. 7 p.m. to 6 a.m. in door-to-door sales or deliveries	
Arkansas	8-48-6	10-54-6	7 p.m. (9 p.m. before non-schoolday) to 6 a.m.	11 p.m. to 6 a.m. before schoolday
California	8-40-6 Schoolday/week: 3-18	8-48-6 Schoolday-week: 4-28 except 8 before non-schoolday. More hours are permitted when school is in session less than 5 days.	7 p.m. (9 p.m. June 1 through Labor Day) to 7 a.m.	10 p.m. (12:30 a.m. before non-schoolday) to 5 a.m.
Colorado	8-40 Schoolday: 6	8-40	9:30 p.m. to 5 a.m. before schoolday	

State or other jurisdiction	Maximum daily and weekly hours and days per week for minors of age:		Nightwork prohibited for minors of age:	
	Under 16	16 and 17	Under 16	16 and 17
Connecticut	8-40-6 in mercantile during periods of school vacation of 5 days or more	Enrolled in and not graduated from a secondary institution. 8-48-6, non-school weeks. Schoolday/week: 6 (8 on Friday, Saturday and Sunday) - 32 in restaurant, recreational, amusement, theater, manufacturing, mechanical, retail, hairdressing, bowling alley, pool hall, or photography gallery establishments. Not enrolled in and not graduated from a secondary institution. 8-48-6 in retail/mercantile establishments. 9-48-6 in restaurant, manufacturing, mechanical, recreation, amusement and theater establishments	7 p.m. (9 p.m. July 1 to the first Monday in September) to 7 a.m.	11 p.m. (midnight if school vacation, not prior to a schoolday, or not attending school) to 6 a.m. in restaurants, recreational, amusement and theater establishments. 10 p.m. (11 p.m. if school vacation, not prior to a school day, or not attending school; midnight in a supermarket of 3,500 square feet or more when no school the next day) to 6 a.m. in manufacturing, mechanical and retail establishments. 10 p.m. to 6 a.m. in hairdressing, bowling alley, pool hall, or photography gallery establishments.

State or other jurisdiction	Maximum daily and weekly hours and days per week for minors of age:		Nightwork prohibited for minors of age:	
	Under 16	16 and 17	Under 16	16 and 17
Delaware	8-40-6 Schoolday/week: 4-18. More hours are permitted when school is in session less than 5 days.	12 (Combined hours of work and school)	7 p.m. (9 p.m. June 1 through Labor Day) to 7 a.m.	8 hours of non-work, non-school time required in each 24-hour day.
Florida	8-40-6 Schoolday: 3 when followed by schoolday, except if enrolled in vocational program Schoolweek: 15 Minors under 16 may work 8-40 during non-school day or week.	8-30-6 during schoolyear	7 p.m. before schoolday to 7 a.m. on schoolday (9 p.m. during holidays and summer vacations to 7 a.m.)	11 p.m. to 6:30 a.m. before schoolday.
Georgia	8-40 Schoolday: 4		9 p.m. to 6 a.m.	
Hawaii	8-40-6 Schoolday: 10 (Combined hours of work and school)		7 p.m. to 7 a.m. (9 p.m. to 6 a.m. June 1 through day before Labor Day).	
Idaho	9-54		9 p.m. to 6 a.m.	
Illinois	8-48-6 Schoolday/week: 3 [8(Combined hours of work and school)] - 24 Eight hours are permitted on both Saturday and Sunday if minor does not work outside school hours more than 6 consecutive days in a week and total hours worked outside school does not exceed 24. Minors age 14 or older, employed in recreational or educational activities by a park district or municipal parks and recreation department may work up to 3 hours per school day twice a week until 9 p.m., while school is in session, if the number of hours worked does not exceed 24 a week. Work is permitted until 10 p.m. during summer vacation.		7 p.m. (9 p.m. June 1 through Labor Day) to 7 a.m. Minors age 14 or older, employed in recreational or educational activities by a park district or municipal parks and recreation department may work up to 3 hours per school day twice a week until 9 p.m., while school is in session, if the number of hours worked does not exceed 24 a week. Work is permitted until 10 p.m. during summer vacation.	

State or other jurisdiction	Maximum daily and weekly hours and days per week for minors of age:		Nightwork prohibited for minors of age:	
	Under 16	16 and 17	Under 16	16 and 17
Indiana	8–40 Schoolday/week: 3-18	8-30 during schoolweek (40 with written parental permission)-6, except if not enrolled in school. 9-30 (48 with written parental permission) during non-school weeks. Applies only to minors enrolled in school	7 p.m. (9 p.m. June 1 through Labor Day) to 7 a.m.	10 p.m. (midnight before non-schoolday with written parental permission) to 6 a.m., minors of 16 enrolled in school. 10 p.m. to 6 a.m. before schoolday, minors of 17 (11:30 p.m. with written parental permission or 1 a.m. with written parental permission up to 2 non-consecutive nights per week).
Iowa	8-40 Schoolday/week: 4-28		7 p.m. (9 p.m. June 1 through Labor Day) to 7 a.m.	
Kansas	8-40		10 p.m. before schoolday to 7 a.m.	
Kentucky	8-40 Schoolday/week: 3 (8 on nonschooldays) -18	6 (8 Saturday and Sunday) 30, if attending school (40 with parental permission and at least a 2.0 school grade point average)	7 p.m. (9 p.m. June 1 through Labor Day) to 7 a.m.	10:30 p.m. (1 a.m. Friday and Saturday) to 6 a.m. when school in session.

State or other jurisdiction	Maximum daily and weekly hours and days per week for minors of age:		Nightwork prohibited for minors of age:	
	Under 16	16 and 17	Under 16	16 and 17
Louisiana	8-40-6 Schoolday/week: 3-18		7 p.m. (9 p.m. June 1 through Labor Day) to 7 a.m. Non-graduate (7 p.m.-7 a.m. on any school day, 9 p.m.-7 a.m. on any non-school day)	Non-graduate 16 year old (11 p.m. - 5 a.m. prior to start of school day) Non-graduate 17 year old (12a.m.-5a.m.) prior to start of any school day.
Maine	8-40-6 Schoolday/week: 3-18 if enrolled in school. Minors under age 18 enrolled in school may work up to 50 hours during any week that school is in session less than 3 days or during the first or last week of the school calendar, regardless of how many days school is in session for the week.	10-50-6 consecutive days if enrolled in school. schoolday/week: 4-20 except 8 before non-schoolday, last scheduled day of school week, on a day on which school is closed. (28 hours in a week with multiple days of school closure) Minors under age 18 enrolled in school may work up to 50 hours during any week that school is in session less than 3 days or during the first or last week of the school calendar, regardless of how many days school is in session for the week.	7 p.m. (9 p.m. during summer vacation) to 7 a.m., if enrolled in school.	10 p.m. (12 a.m. before non-schoolday) to 7 a.m. if enrolled in school. 5 a.m. before non-schoolday.

State or other jurisdiction	Maximum daily and weekly hours and days per week for minors of age:		Nightwork prohibited for minors of age:	
	Under 16	16 and 17	Under 16	16 and 17
Maryland	8-40 Schoolday/week: 4-23, More hours are permitted when school is in session less than 5 days.	12 (Combined hours of work and school)	8 p.m. (9 p.m. Memorial Day through Labor Day) to 7 a.m.	8 consecutive hours of non-work, non-schoolday time required in each 24-hour day.
Massachusetts	8-48-6	9-48-6	7 p.m. (9 p.m. July 1 through Labor Day) to 6:30 a.m.	10 p.m. (midnight in restaurants and at race tracks on Friday, Saturday, and vacation) to 6 a.m.
Michigan	10-48-6 Schoolweek: 48 (Combined hours of work and school)	10-48-6 Schoolweek: 48 (Combined hours of work and school)	9 p.m. to 7 a.m.	10:30 p.m. (11:30 p.m. on Fridays, Saturdays and during school vacations) to 6 a.m., if attending school. 11:30 p.m. to 6 a.m., if not attending school.
Minnesota	8-40		9 p.m. to 7 a.m.	11 p.m. to 5 a.m. before schoolday (11:30 p.m. to 4:30 a.m. with written parental permission).
Mississippi	8-44 in factory, mill, cannery or workshop.		7 p.m. to 6 a.m. in factory, mill, cannery or workshop.	
Missouri	8-40-6 Schoolday: 3		7 p.m. (9 p.m. June 1 through Labor Day 10:30 p.m. at regional Fairs or expositions) to 7 a.m.	

State or other jurisdiction	Maximum daily and weekly hours and days per week for minors of age:		Nightwork prohibited for minors of age:	
	Under 16	16 and 17	Under 16	16 and 17
Montana	8-40 Schoolday/week: 3-18 Students of 14 and 15 enrolled in approved Work Experience and Career Exploration programs may work during school hours up to 3 hours on a schoolday and 23 hours in a schoolweek.		7 p.m. (9 p.m. during periods outside the school year (June 1 through Labor Day, depending on local standards)) to 7 a.m.	
Nebraska	8-48		8 p.m. to 6 a.m., under 14. 10 p.m. (beyond 10 p.m. before non-schoolday with special permit) to 6 a.m., 14 and 15.	
Nevada	8-48		---	
New Hampshire	8 on non-schoolday, 48-hour week during vacation, if enrolled in school. Schoolday/week: 3-23 if enrolled in school.	48-hour week, 6-day week, during vacation, if enrolled in school. 30-hour week, 6-day week, if enrolled in school.	9 p.m. to 7 a.m.	
New Jersey	8-40-6 Schoolday/week: 3-18	8-40-6	7 p.m. (9 p.m. during summer vacation with parental permission) to 7 a.m.	11 p.m. to 6 a.m. during school term, with specified variations
New Mexico	8-44 (48 in special cases), under 14		9 p.m. to 7 a.m., under 14	

State or other jurisdiction	Maximum daily and weekly hours and days per week for minors of age:		Nightwork prohibited for minors of age:	
	Under 16	16 and 17	Under 16	16 and 17
New York	8-40-6 Schoolday/week: 3-18. Students of 14 and 15 enrolled in approved Work Experience and Career Exploration programs may work during school hours up to 3 hours on a schoolday and 23 hours in a schoolweek.	8-48-6 Schoolday/week: 4 before schoolday, 8 Friday, Saturday, Sunday or holiday-28, if enrolled in school.	7 p.m. (9 p.m. June 21 through Labor Day) to 7 a.m.	10 p.m. (midnight before schooldays with written permission from both parent and school and before non-schoolday with written parental consent) to 6 a.m., while school is in session. Midnight to 6 a.m. while school is not in session.
North Carolina	8-40 Schoolday/week: 3-18. Students of 14 and 15 enrolled in approved Work Experience and Career Exploration programs may work during school hours up to 3 hours on a schoolday and 23 hours in a schoolweek.		7 p.m. (9 p.m. during summer vacation) to 7 a.m.	11 p.m. to 5 a.m. before schoolday while school is in session. Not applicable with written permission from both parent and school.
North Dakota	8-40-6 Schoolday/week: 3-18 if not exempted from school attendance.	8-48-6	7 p.m. (9 p.m. June 1 through Labor Day) to 7 a.m.	
Ohio	8-40 Schoolday/week: 3-18		7 p.m. (9 p.m. June 1 to Sept. 1 and during school holidays of 5 schooldays or more) to 7 a.m., 7 p.m. to 7 a.m. in door-to-door sales.	11 p.m. before schoolday to 7 a.m. on schoolday (6 a.m. if not employed after 8 p.m. previous night) if required to attend school. 8 p.m. to 7 a.m. in door-to-door sales.

State or other jurisdiction	Maximum daily and weekly hours and days per week for minors of age:		Nightwork prohibited for minors of age:	
	Under 16	16 and 17	Under 16	16 and 17
Oklahoma	8-40 Schoolday/week: 3-18 8 hours on schooldays before non-schooldays if employer not covered by FLSA		7 p.m. (9 p.m. June 1 through Labor Day) to 7 a.m. 9 p.m. before non-schooldays if employer not covered by FLSA	
Oregon	8-40 Schoolday/week: 3-18 Students of 14 and 15 enrolled in approved Work Experience and Career Exploration programs may work during school hours up to 3 hours on a schoolday and 23 hours in a schoolweek.	44-hour week (emergency overtime with permit)	7 p.m. (9 p.m. June 1 through Labor Day) to 7 a.m.	
Pennsylvania	8-44-6 Schoolday/week: 4 (8 on non-schoolday) -18	8-44-6 28 in schoolweek, if enrolled in regular day school	7 p.m. (10 p.m. during vacation from June to Labor Day) to 7 a.m.	12 p.m. (1 a.m. before non-schoolday) to 6 a.m., if enrolled in regular day school.
Rhode Island	8-40	9-48, during school year	7 p.m. (9 p.m. during school vacation) to 6 a.m.	11:30 p.m. (1:30 a.m. before non-schoolday) to 6 a.m., if regularly attending school.
South Carolina	8-40 Schoolday/week: 3-18		7 p.m. (9 p.m. June 1 through Labor Day) to 7 a.m.	
South Dakota	8-40 Schoolday/week: 4-20		After 10 p.m. before schoolday	
Tennessee	8-40 Schoolday/week: 3-18		7 p.m. to 7 a.m. (9 p.m. to 6 a.m. before non-schooldays)	10 p.m. to 6 a.m. (Sunday - Thursday before schooldays) (midnight with parental permission up to 3 nights a week)

State or other jurisdiction	Maximum daily and weekly hours and days per week for minors of age:		Nightwork prohibited for minors of age:	
	Under 16	16 and 17	Under 16	16 and 17
Texas	8-48		10 p.m. (midnight before non-schoolday or in summer if not enrolled in summer school) to 5 a.m.	
Utah	8-40 Schoolday: 4		9:30 p.m. to 5 a.m. before schoolday.	
Vermont	8-40-6, non-schoolday period. Schoolday/week: 3-18		7 p.m. (9 p.m. June 1 through Labor Day) to 7 a.m.	
Virginia	8-40, non-school period. Schoolday/week: 3-18		7 p.m. (9 p.m. June 1 through Labor Day) to 7 a.m.	
Washington	8-40-6 Schoolday/week: 3 (8 Friday, Saturday and Sunday) - 16	8-48-6 Schoolday/week: 4 (8 Friday, Saturday and Sunday) - 20. 6-28 with special variance agreed to by parent, employer, student and school	7 p.m. (9 p.m. Friday and Saturday when school is not in session) to 7 a.m.	10 p.m. Sunday - Thursday (midnight Friday and Saturday and when school is not in session) to 7 a.m. (5 a.m. when school is not in session). 9 p.m. to 7 a.m. in door-to-door sales.
West Virginia	No minor under 16 years of age may work during school hours under any circumstances.		7 p.m. (9 p.m. June 1 through Labor Day) to 7 a.m.. Supervision permit may be issued allowing 14 and 15 year old minors to work until 11:00p.m. when school is not in session.	

State or other jurisdiction	Maximum daily and weekly hours and days per week for minors of age:		Nightwork prohibited for minors of age:	
	Under 16	16 and 17	Under 16	16 and 17
Wisconsin	8-40-6 Schoolday/week: 4 (8 last schoolday of week and non-schoolday) – 18 More hours are permitted when school is in session less than 5 days.	See Below-50-6 Schoolday/week: 5 (8 last schoolday of week and non-schoolday) -26 More hours are permitted when school is in session less than 5 days. has no limit during non-school week on daily hours or nightwork for 16- and 17-year-olds. However, they must be paid time and one-half for work in excess of 10 hours per day or 40 hours per week, whichever is greater. Also, 8 hours rest is required between end of work and start of work the next day, and any work between 12:30 a.m. and 5 a.m. must be directly supervised by an adult.	8 p.m. (11 p.m. before non-schoolday) to 7 a.m.	11 p.m. (12:30 a.m. before non-schoolday) to 7 a.m. (5 a.m. on non-schoolday during schoolweek. No limit during non-school week on daily hours or nightwork for 16-and 17-year-olds. However, they must be paid time and one-half for work in excess of 10 hours per day or 40 hours per week, whichever is greater. Also, 8 hours rest is required between end of work and start of work the next day, and any work between 12:30 a.m. and 5 a.m. must be directly supervised by an adult.

State or other jurisdiction	Maximum daily and weekly hours and days per week for minors of age:		Nightwork prohibited for minors of age:	
	Under 16	16 and 17	Under 16	16 and 17
Wyoming	8-56		10 p.m. (midnight before non-schoolday and for minors not enrolled in school) to 5 a.m.	Midnight to 5 a.m., female
District of Columbia	8-48-6	8-48-6	7 p.m. (9 p.m. June 1 through Labor Day) to 7 a.m.	10 p.m. to 6 a.m.
Guam	8-40-6 Schoolday: 9 (Combined hours of work and school)	8-40-6 Schoolday: 9 (Combined hours of work and school)	10 p.m. (midnight on non-school nights) to 6 a.m.	10 p.m. (midnight on non-school nights) to 6 a.m.
Puerto Rico	8-40-6 Schoolday: 8 (Combined hours of work and school)	8-40-6	6 p.m. to 8 a.m.	10 p.m. to 6 a.m.

APPENDIX 5 – MINIMUM WAGES FOR TIPPED EMPLOYEES – EFFECTIVE JANUARY 1, 2013

Jurisdiction	Basic Combined Cash & Tip Minimum Wage Rate	Maximum Tip Credit Against Minimum Wage	Minimum Cash Wage — Other additional deductions are permitted, for example for meals and lodging, except in WI	Definition of Tipped Employee by Minimum Tips received (monthly unless otherwise specified)
FEDERAL: Fair Labor Standards Act (FLSA)	$7.25	$5.12	$2.13	More than $30
Alaska			$7.75	
California			$8.00	
Guam			$6.55	
Minnesota:				
Large employer - A large employer is an enterprise with annual receipts of $625,000 or more; a small employer, less than $625,000.			$6.15	
Small employer			$5.25	
Montana:			$7.65	
Business with gross annual sales over $110,000				
Business with gross annual sales of $110,000 or less			$4.00	

Jurisdiction	Basic Combined Cash & Tip Minimum Wage Rate	Maximum Tip Credit Against Minimum Wage	Minimum Cash Wage — Other additional deductions are permitted, for example for meals and lodging, except in WI	Definition of Tipped Employee by Minimum Tips received (monthly unless otherwise specified)
Nevada			$8.25	With no health insurance benefits provided by employer and received by employee
			$7.25	With health insurance benefits provided by employer and received by employee
Oregon			$8.95	
Washington			$9.19	
Puerto Rico				
Arizona	$7.80	$3.00	$4.80	Not specified
Arkansas	$6.25	$3.62	$2.63	More than $20
Colorado	$7.78	$3.02	$4.76	More than $30
Connecticut	$8.25	31.0%	$5.69	At least $10 weekly for full-time employees or $2.00 daily for part-time in hotels and restaurants. Not specified for other industries.
Hotel, restaurant		$2.56	$5.69	
Bartenders who customarily receive tips		11%	$7.34	
Delaware	$7.25	$5.02	$2.23	More than $30
District of Columbia	$8.25	$5.48	$2.77	Not specified

Jurisdiction	Basic Combined Cash & Tip Minimum Wage Rate	Maximum Tip Credit Against Minimum Wage	Minimum Cash Wage Other additional deductions are permitted, for example for meals and lodging, except in WI	Definition of Tipped Employee by Minimum Tips received (monthly unless otherwise specified)
Florida	$7.79	$3.02	$4.77	
Hawaii	$7.25	$0.25	$7.00	More than $20
Idaho	$7.25	$3.90	$3.35	More than $30
Illinois	$8.25	40%	$4.95	$20
Indiana	$7.25	$5.12	$2.13	Not specified
Iowa	$7.25	$2.90	$4.35	More than $30
Kansas	$7.25	$5.12	$2.13	More than $20
Kentucky	$7.25	$5.12	$2.13	More than $30
Maine	$7.50	50%	$3.75	More than $20
Maryland	$7.25	$3.62	$3.63	More than $30
Massachusetts	$8.00	$5.37	$2.63	More than $20
Michigan	$7.40	$4.75	$2.65	Not specified
Missouri	$7.35	$3.675	$3.675	Not specified
Nebraska	$7.25	$5.12	$2.13	Not specified
New Hampshire	$7.25	55%	45%	More than $30

Jurisdiction	Basic Combined Cash & Tip Minimum Wage Rate	Maximum Tip Credit Against Minimum Wage	Minimum Cash Wage Other additional deductions are permitted, for example for meals and lodging, except in WI	Definition of Tipped Employee by Minimum Tips received (monthly unless otherwise specified)
New Jersey The listed maximum credit is the total amount allowable for tips, food and lodging combined, not for tips alone as in other states. In specific situations where the employer can prove to the satisfaction of the labor department that the tips actually received exceed the creditable amount, a higher tip credit may be taken.	$7.25	$5.12	$2.13	Not specified
New Mexico	$7.50	$5.37	$2.13	More than $30
New York *Food service workers* *Service Employees in All Establishments* *Service Employees in Resort Hotels if tips at least $4.10 per hour*	$7.25	$2.25 $1.60 $2.35	$5.00 $5.65 $4.90	Not specified
North Carolina Tip credit is not permitted unless the employer obtains from each employee, monthly or for each pay period, a signed certification of the amount of tips received.	$7.25	$5.12	$2.13	More than $20

Jurisdiction	Basic Combined Cash & Tip Minimum Wage Rate	Maximum Tip Credit Against Minimum Wage	Minimum Cash Wage — Other additional deductions are permitted, for example for meals and lodging, except in WI	Definition of Tipped Employee by Minimum Tips received (monthly unless otherwise specified)
North Dakota	$7.25	33%	$4.86	More than $30
Ohio — The minimum cash wage for tipped employees of employers with gross annual sales in excess of $255,000 is $3.50 per hour (plus tips). For tipped employees of employers with gross annual sales of less than $255,000, the tipped employee hourly rate is $2.93 per hour (plus tips).	$7.85	$3.92	$3.93	More than $30
Oklahoma — The listed maximum credit is the total amount allowable for tips, food and lodging combined, not for tips alone as in other states. When a food and/or lodging credit is not involved, the wage tip credit is limited to $2.13 per hour. For employers with fewer than 10 full-time employees at any one location who have gross annual sales of $100,000 or less, the basic minimum rate is $2.00 per hour, with a 50% maximum tip credit.	$7.25	$3.62 or 50% 3	$3.63	Not specified

Jurisdiction	Basic Combined Cash & Tip Minimum Wage Rate	Maximum Tip Credit Against Minimum Wage	Minimum Cash Wage Other additional deductions are permitted, for example for meals and lodging, except in WI	Definition of Tipped Employee by Minimum Tips received (monthly unless otherwise specified)
Pennsylvania	$7.25	$4.42	$2.83	More than $30
Rhode Island	$7.75	$4.86	$2.89	Not specified
South Dakota The listed maximum credit is the total amount allowable for tips, food and lodging combined, not for tips alone as in other states.	$7.25	$5.12	$2.13	More than $35
Texas	$7.25	$5.12	$2.13	More than $20
Utah	$7.25	$5.12	$2.13	More than $30
Vermont Employees in hotels, motels, tourist places, and restaurants who customarily and regularly receive tips for direct and personal customer service.	$8.60	$4.43	$4.17	More than $120
Virginia	$7.25	$5.12	$2.13	Not specified
Virgin Islands	$7.25	$5.12	$2.13	Not specified
West Virginia For employers with six or more employees and for state agencies.	$7.25	20%	$5.80	Not specified

Jurisdiction	Basic Combined Cash & Tip Minimum Wage Rate	Maximum Tip Credit Against Minimum Wage	Minimum Cash Wage — Other additional deductions are permitted, for example for meals and lodging, except in WI	Definition of Tipped Employee by Minimum Tips received (monthly unless otherwise specified)
Wisconsin $2.13 per hour may be paid to employees who are not yet 20 years old and who have been in employment status with a particular employer for 90 or fewer consecutive calendar days from the date of initial employment.	$7.25	$4.92	$2.33	Not specified
Wyoming	$5.15	$3.02	$2.13	More than $30

Appendix 6 - Minimum Length of Meal Period Required Under State Law For Adult Employees in Private Sector - Effective January 1, 2013

Jurisdiction	Basic Standard	Coverage (Not displayed in table are exemptions for executive, administrative and professional employees, and for outside salespersons)	Comments
Alabama			This jurisdiction has separate provisions requiring meal periods specifically for minors (when minors are covered by two provisions, employer must observe the higher standard).
Alaska			This jurisdiction has separate provisions requiring meal periods specifically for minors (when minors are covered by two provisions, employer must observe the higher standard).
California	½ hour, after 5 hours, except when workday will be completed in 6 hours or less and there is mutual employer/employee consent to waive meal period. On-duty meal period counted as time worked and permitted only when nature of work prevents relief from all duties and there is written agreement between parties. Employee may revoke agreement at any time. An employer may not employ an employee for a work period of more than 10 hours per day without providing the employee with a second meal period of not less than 30 minutes, except that if the total hours worked is no more than 12 hours, the second meal period may be waived by mutual consent of the employer and employee only if the first meal period was not waived. The Industrial Welfare Commission may adopt working condition orders permitting a meal period to start after 6 hours of work if the commission determines that the order is consistent with the health and welfare of the affected employees.	Uniform application to industries under 14 Orders, including agriculture and private household employment. Exempts employees in the wholesale baking industry who are subject to an Industrial Welfare Commission Wage Order and who are covered by a valid collective bargaining agreement that provides for a 35-hour workweek consisting of five 7-hour days, payment of 1 and ½ times the regular rate of pay for time worked in excess of 7 hours per day, and a rest period of not less than 10 minutes every 2 hours. Exceptions apply to motion picture or broadcasting industries pursuant to Labor Code sections 512 and 226.7, and Industrial Welfare Commission Wage Orders 11 and 12.	This jurisdiction also has separate provisions requiring meal periods specifically for minors (when minors are covered by two provisions, employer must observe the higher standard). This jurisdiction also has rest period requirements.

Jurisdiction	Basic Standard	Coverage	Comments
		(Not displayed in table are exemptions for executive, administrative and professional employees, and for outside salespersons)	
Colorado	½ hour after 5 hours, except when workday will be completed in 6 hours or less. On-duty meal period counted as time worked and permitted when nature of work prevents relief from all duties.	Applicable to retail trade, food and beverage, public housekeeping, medical profession, beauty service, laundry and dry cleaning, and janitorial service industries. Excludes certain occupations, such as teacher, nurse, and other medical professionals.	This jurisdiction also has separate provisions requiring meal periods specifically for minors (when minors are covered by two provisions, employer must observe the higher standard). This jurisdiction also has rest period requirements.
Connecticut	½ hour after first 2 hours and before last 2 hours for employees who work 7½ consecutive hours or more.	Excludes employer who provides 30 or more total minutes of paid rest or meal periods within each 7½ hour work period. Meal period requirement does not alter or impair collective bargaining agreement in effect on 7/1/90, or prevent a different schedule by written employer/employee agreement.	Labor Commissioner is directed to exempt by regulation any employer on a finding that compliance would be adverse to public safety, or that duties of a position can be performed only by one employee, or in continuous operations under specified conditions, or that employer employs less than 5 employees on a shift at a single place of business provided the exemption applies only to employees on such shift.

Jurisdiction	Basic Standard	Coverage *(Not displayed in table are exemptions for executive, administrative and professional employees, and for outside salespersons)*	Comments
Delaware	½ hour, after first 2 hours and before the last 2 hours, for employees who work 7½ consecutive hours or more.	Excludes teachers and workplaces covered by a collective bargaining agreement or other written employer/ employee agreement providing otherwise. Exemptions may also be granted where compliance would adversely affect public safety; only one employee may perform the duties of a position, an employer has fewer than five employees on a shift at a single place of business; or where the continuous nature of an employer's operations requires employees to respond to urgent or unusual conditions at all times and the employees are compensated for their meal break periods.	An administrative penalty of up to $1,000 for each violation may be assessed an employer who discharges or discriminates against an employee for complaining or providing information to the Department of Labor pursuant to a violation of this requirement. This jurisdiction also has separate provisions requiring meal periods specifically for minors (when minors are covered by two provisions, employer must observe the higher standard).
Florida			This jurisdiction has separate provisions requiring meal periods specifically for minors (when minors are covered by two provisions, employer must observe the higher standard).
Hawaii			This jurisdiction has separate provisions requiring meal periods specifically for minors (when minors are covered by two provisions, employer must observe the higher standard).

Jurisdiction	Basic Standard	Coverage (Not displayed in table are exemptions for executive, administrative and professional employees, and for outside salespersons)	Comments
Illinois	Each hotel room attendant -- those persons who clean or put guest rooms in order in a hotel or other establishment licensed for transient occupancy -- shall receive a minimum of two 15-minute paid rest breaks and one 30-minute meal period in each workday in which they work at least seven hours.	Applies to an establishment located in a county with a population greater than three million. Excludes employees whose meal periods are established by collective bargaining. Different requirements apply to employees who monitor individuals with developmental disabilities and/or mental illness.	Employees may not be required to work during a break period. Break area must be provided with adequate seating and tables in a clean and comfortable environment. Clean drinking water must be provided without charge. Employer must keep complete and accurate records of the break periods. This jurisdiction also has separate provisions requiring meal periods specifically for minors (when minors are covered by two provisions, employer must observe the higher standard).
Indiana			This jurisdiction has separate provisions requiring meal periods specifically for minors (when minors are covered by two provisions, employer must observe the higher standard).
Iowa			This jurisdiction has separate provisions requiring meal periods specifically for minors (when minors are covered by two provisions, employer must observe the higher standard).

Jurisdiction	Basic Standard	Coverage (Not displayed in table are exemptions for executive, administrative and professional employees, and for outside salespersons)	Comments
Kentucky	Reasonable off-duty period, ordinarily ½ hour but shorter period permitted under special conditions, between 3rd and 5th hour of work. Not counted as time worked. Coffee breaks and snack time not to be included in meal period.	Excludes employers subject to Federal Railway Labor Act. Meal period requirement does not negate collective bargaining agreement or mutual agreement between employer and employee.	This jurisdiction also has separate provisions requiring meal periods specifically for minors (when minors are covered by two provisions, employer must observe the higher standard). This jurisdiction also has rest period requirements.
Louisiana			This jurisdiction has separate provisions requiring meal periods specifically for minors (when minors are covered by two provisions, employer must observe the higher standard).
Maryland			This jurisdiction has separate provisions requiring meal periods specifically for minors (when minors are covered by two provisions, employer must observe the higher standard).
Maine	½ hour, after 6 consecutive hours, except in cases of emergency and except where nature of work allows employees frequent breaks during workday.	Applicable to places of employment where 3 or more employees are on duty at one time. Not applicable if collective bargaining or other written employer-employee agreement provides otherwise.	

Jurisdiction	Basic Standard	Coverage *(Not displayed in table are exemptions for executive, administrative and professional employees, and for outside salespersons)*	Comments
Massachusetts	½ hour, if work is for more than 6 hours.	Excludes iron works, glass works, paper mills, letter press establishments, print works, and bleaching or dyeing works.	Labor Commissioner may grant exemption to a factory workshop or mechanical establishment, if in discretion of Commissioner, it is necessary by reason of continuous process or special circumstance, including collective bargaining agreement. This jurisdiction also has separate provisions requiring meal periods specifically for minors (when minors are covered by two provisions, employer must observe the higher standard).
Michigan			This jurisdiction has separate provisions requiring meal periods specifically for minors (when minors are covered by two provisions, employer must observe the higher standard).
Minnesota	Sufficient unpaid time for employees who work 8 consecutive hours or more.	Excludes certain agricultural and seasonal employees. Meal period requirement does not prohibit different provisions under collective bargaining agreement.	This jurisdiction also has separate provisions requiring meal periods specifically for minors (when minors are covered by two provisions, employer must observe the higher standard). This jurisdiction also has rest period requirements.

Jurisdiction	Basic Standard	Coverage (Not displayed in table are exemptions for executive, administrative and professional employees, and for outside salespersons)	Comments
Nebraska	½ hour, off premises, between 12 noon and 1 p.m. or at other suitable lunch time.	Applicable to assembly plant, workshop, or mechanical establishment, unless employee is covered by a valid collective bargaining agreement or other written agreement between an employer and employee.	This jurisdiction also has separate provisions requiring meal periods specifically for minors (when minors are covered by two provisions, employer must observe the higher standard).
Nevada	½ hour, if work is for 8 continuous hours.	Applicable to employers of two or more employees. Excludes employees covered by collective bargaining agreement	Labor Commissioner may grant exemption on employer evidence of business necessity. This jurisdiction also has separate provisions requiring meal periods specifically for minors (when minors are covered by two provisions, employer must observe the higher standard). This jurisdiction also has rest period requirements.
New Hampshire	½ hour, after 5 consecutive hours, unless feasible for employee to eat while working and is permitted to do so by employer.	Applicable to any employer.	This jurisdiction also has separate provisions requiring meal periods specifically for minors (when minors are covered by two provisions, employer must observe the higher standard).

Jurisdiction	Basic Standard	Coverage *(Not displayed in table are exemptions for executive, administrative and professional employees, and for outside salespersons)*	Comments
New Jersey			This jurisdiction has separate provisions requiring meal periods specifically for minors (when minors are covered by two provisions, employer must observe the higher standard).
New Mexico			A provision applicable to females and administratively extended to men does not require a meal period, but provides that when a meal period is granted (in industrial, mercantile and certain service industries), it must be at least ½ hour, not counted as time worked.
New York	1 hour noon-day period 30 minute noonday period for employees who work shifts of more than 6 hours that extend over the noon day meal period. An additional 20 minutes between 5 p.m. and 7 p.m. for those employed on a shift starting before 11 a.m. and continuing after 7 p.m. 1 hour in factories, 45 minutes in other establishments, midway in shift, for those employed more than a 6-hour period starting between 1 p.m. and 6 a.m.	Factories All other establishments and occupations covered by the Labor Law. All industries and occupations. See basic standard	Labor Commissioner may give written permission for shorter meal period under each standard. This jurisdiction also has separate provisions requiring meal periods specifically for minors (when minors are covered by two provisions, employer must observe the higher standard).

Jurisdiction	Basic Standard	Coverage (Not displayed in table are exemptions for executive, administrative and professional employees, and for outside salespersons)	Comments
North Carolina			This jurisdiction has separate provisions requiring meal periods specifically for minors (when minors are covered by two provisions, employer must observe the higher standard).
North Dakota	½ hour, if desired, on each shift exceeding 5 hours.	Applicable when two or more employees are on duty. Collective bargaining agreement takes precedence over meal period requirement.	Employees who are completely relieved of their duties but required to remain on site do not have to be paid. This jurisdiction also has separate provisions requiring meal periods specifically for minors (when minors are covered by two provisions, employer must observe the higher standard).
Ohio			This jurisdiction has separate provisions requiring meal periods specifically for minors (when minors are covered by two provisions, employer must observe the higher standard).
Oklahoma			This jurisdiction has separate provisions requiring meal periods specifically for minors (when minors are covered by two provisions, employer must observe the higher standard).

Jurisdiction	Basic Standard	Coverage *(Not displayed in table are exemptions for executive, administrative and professional employees, and for outside salespersons)*	Comments
Oregon	½ hour, with relief from all duty, for each work period of 6 to 8 hours, between 2nd and 5th hour for work period of 7 hours or less and between 3rd and 6th hour for work period over 7 hours; or, less than ½ hour but not less than 20 minutes, with pay, with relief from all duty, where employer can show that such a paid meal period is industry practice or custom; or, where employer can show that nature of work prevents relief from all duty, an eating period with pay while on duty for each period of 6 to 8 hours.	Applicable to every employer, except in agriculture and except employees covered by collective bargaining agreement.	In absence of regularly scheduled meal periods, it is sufficient compliance when employer can show that the employee has, in fact, received the time specified (permitted only where employer can show that ordinary nature of the work prevents employer from establishing and maintaining a regularly scheduled meal period). This jurisdiction also has separate provisions requiring meal periods specifically for minors (when minors are covered by two provisions, employer must observe the higher standard). This jurisdiction also has rest period requirements.
Pennsylvania			This jurisdiction has separate provisions requiring meal periods specifically for minors (when minors are covered by two provisions, employer must observe the higher standard). A 30-minute meal period is required for seasonal farm workers after 5 hours.

Jurisdiction	Basic Standard	Coverage (Not displayed in table are exemptions for executive, administrative and professional employees, and for outside salespersons)	Comments
Rhode Island	All employees are entitled to a 20 minute mealtime within a six hour work shift, and a 30 minute mealtime within an eight hour work shift.	Uniform application to all employees except to an employer of a licensed health care facility or an employer who employs less than three people on any shift at the worksite.	This jurisdiction also has separate provisions requiring meal periods specifically for minors (when minors are covered by two provisions, employer must observe the higher standard).
Tennessee	½ hour for employees scheduled to work 6 consecutive hours or more.	Applicable to every employer.	
Utah			This jurisdiction has separate provisions requiring meal periods specifically for minors (when minors are covered by two provisions, employer must observe the higher standard).
Vermont	Employees are to be given "reasonable opportunities" during work periods to eat and use toilet facilities in order to protect the health and hygiene of the employee.	Universal application	
Virginia			This jurisdiction has separate provisions requiring meal periods specifically for minors (when minors are covered by two provisions, employer must observe the higher standard).

Jurisdiction	Basic Standard	Coverage *(Not displayed in table are exemptions for executive, administrative and professional employees, and for outside salespersons)*	Comments
Washington	½ hour, if work period is more than 5 consecutive hours, to be given not less than 2 hours nor more than 5 hours from beginning of shift. Counted as work time if employee is required to remain on duty on premises or at a prescribed worksite. Additional ½ hour, before or during overtime, for employees working 3 or more hours beyond regular workday.	Excludes newspaper vendor or carrier, domestic or casual labor around private residence, sheltered workshop, and agricultural labor. Rules for construction trade employees may be superseded by a collective bargaining agreement covering such employees if the terms of the agreement specifically require meal periods and prescribe requirements concerning them.	Director of Labor and Industries may grant variance for good cause, upon employer application. This jurisdiction also has separate provisions requiring meal periods specifically for minors (when minors are covered by two provisions, employer must observe the higher standard). A 30-minute meal period after 5 hours is required in agriculture and an additional 30 minutes for employees working 11 or more hours in a day. This jurisdiction also has rest period requirements.
West Virginia	20 minutes for employees who work 6 consecutive hours or more.	Applicable to every employer. Meal period is required where employees are not afforded necessary breaks and/or permitted to eat lunch while working.	This jurisdiction also has separate provisions requiring meal periods specifically for minors (when minors are covered by two provisions, employer must observe the higher standard).

Jurisdiction	Basic Standard	Coverage *(Not displayed in table are exemptions for executive, administrative and professional employees, and for outside salespersons)*	Comments
Wisconsin			This jurisdiction has separate provisions requiring meal periods specifically for minors (when minors are covered by two provisions, employer must observe the higher standard). A 30-minute meal period is required for migrant workers after 6 hours. By regulation, the recommended standard is ½ hour after 6 consecutive hours' work in factories, mechanical and mercantile establishments and certain service industries, to be given reasonably close to usual meal time or near middle of shift.
Guam	½ hour, after 5 hours, except when workday will be completed in 6 hours or less and there is mutual employer/employee consent to waive meal period. Not considered time worked unless nature of work prevents relief from duty.	Excludes agriculture where fewer than 10 are employed, domestic employment, and fishing industry, among others.	This jurisdiction also has separate provisions requiring meal periods specifically for minors (when minors are covered by two provisions, employer must observe the higher standard).

Jurisdiction	Basic Standard	Coverage *(Not displayed in table are exemptions for executive, administrative and professional employees, and for outside salespersons)*	Comments
Puerto Rico	1 hour, after end of 3rd but before beginning of 6th consecutive hour worked. Double-time pay required for work during meal hour or fraction thereof.	Excludes domestic service; and public sector employment other than agricultural, industrial, commercial or public service enterprises.	Meal period may be shortened for convenience of employee by mutual employer/employee consent and with approval of Secretary of Labor. Such consent and approval not necessary if union and employer agree on shorter period. Requirement for a second meal period for employees working up to 10 hours may be waived with approval of Secretary of Labor. This jurisdiction also has separate provisions requiring meal periods specifically for minors (when minors are covered by two provisions, employer must observe the higher standard).

Appendix 7 - Minimum Paid Rest Period Requirements Under State Law for Adult Employees in Private Sector – Effective January 1, 2013

Alabama

None

Alaska

None

Arizona

None

Arkansas

None

California

- *Paid 10-minute rest period for each 4 hours worked or major fraction thereof; as practicable, in middle of each work period. Not required for employees whose total daily work time is less than 3 and ½ hours.*

- *Uniform application to industries under 15 Orders, including agriculture and household employment.*

- *Excludes professional actors, sheepherders under Agricultural Occupations Order, and personal attendants under Household Occupations Order.*

- *Additional interim rest periods required in motion picture industry during actual rehearsal or shooting for swimmers, dancers, skaters or other performers engaged in strenuous physical activity.*

- *Under all Orders, except for private household employment, Division of Labor Standards Enforcement may grant exemption upon employer application on the basis of undue hardship, if exemption would not materially affect welfare or comfort of employees.*

- *This jurisdiction also has meal period requirements.*

Colorado

- *Paid 10-minute rest period for each 4-hour work period or major fraction thereof; as practicable, in middle of each work period.*

- *Applicable to retail trade, food and beverage, public housekeeping, medical profession, beauty service, laundry and dry cleaning and janitorial service industries. Excludes certain occupations, such as teacher, nurse, and other medical professionals.*

- *This jurisdiction also has meal period requirements.*

Connecticut

None

Delaware

None

Florida

None

Georgia

None

Hawaii

None

Idaho

None

Illinois

- *Each hotel room attendant -- those persons who clean or put guest rooms in order in a hotel or other establishment licensed for transient occupancy -- shall receive a minimum of two 15-minute paid rest breaks and one 30-minute meal period in each workday in which they work at least seven hours.*

- *Applies to an establishment located in a county with a population greater than three million.*

- *Employees may not be required to work during a break period. Break area must be provided with adequate seating and tables in a clean and comfortable environment. Clean drinking water must be provided without charge. Employer must keep complete and accurate records of the break periods.*

- *This jurisdiction also has meal period requirements.*

Indiana

None

Iowa

None

Kansas

None

Kentucky

- *Paid 10-minute rest period for each 4-hour work period.*

- *Excludes employees under the Federal Railway Labor Act.*

- *Rest period must be in addition to regularly scheduled meal period.*

- *This jurisdiction also has meal period requirements.*

Louisiana

None

Maine

None

Maryland

None

Massachusetts

None

Michigan

None

Minnesota

- *Paid adequate rest period within each 4 consecutive hours of work, to utilize nearest convenient restroom.*

- *Excludes certain agricultural and seasonal employees.*

- *Different rest breaks permitted if pursuant to a collective bargaining agreement.*

- *This jurisdiction also has meal period requirements.*

Mississippi

None

Missouri

None

Montana

None

Nebraska

None

Nevada

- *Paid 10-minute rest period for each 4 hours worked or major fraction thereof; as practicable, in middle of each work period. Not required for employees whose total daily work time is less than 3 and ½ hours.*

- *Applicable to employers of two or more employees at a particular place of employment.*

- *Excludes employees covered by a collective bargaining agreement.*

- *Labor Commissioner may grant exemption on employer evidence of business necessity.*

- *This jurisdiction also has meal period requirements.*

New Hampshire

None

New Jersey

None

New Mexico

None

New York

None

North Carolina

None

North Dakota

None

Ohio

None

Oklahoma

None

Oregon

- *Paid 10-minute rest period for every 4-hour segment or major portion thereof in one work period; as feasible, approximately in middle of each segment of work period.*

- *Applicable to every employer, except in agriculture and except employees covered by collective bargaining agreement.*

- *Rest period must be in addition to usual meal period and taken separately; not to be added to usual meal period or deducted from beginning or end of work period to reduce overall length of total work period.*

In absence of regularly scheduled rest periods, it is sufficient compliance when employer can show that the employee has, in fact, received the time specified (permitted only where employer can show that ordinary nature of the work prevents employer from establishing and maintaining a regularly scheduled rest period).

Rest period is not required for employees age 18 or older who work alone in a retail or service establishment serving the general public and who work less than 5 hours in a period of 16 continuous hours.

- *This jurisdiction also has meal period requirements.*

Pennsylvania

None

Rhode Island

None

South Carolina

None

South Dakota

None

Tennessee

None

Texas

None

Utah

None

Vermont

- *Employees are to be given "reasonable opportunities" during work periods to eat and use toilet facilities in order to protect the health and hygiene of the employee.*

Virginia

None

Washington

- *Paid 10-minute rest period for each 4-hour work period, scheduled as near as possible to midpoint of each work period. Employee may not be required to work more than 3 hours without a rest period.*

- *Excludes newspaper vendor or carrier, domestic or casual labor around private residence, sheltered workshop, and agricultural labor.*

- *Rules for construction trade employees may be superseded by a collective bargaining agreement covering such employees if the terms of the agreement specifically require rest periods and prescribe requirements concerning them.*

- *Scheduled rest periods not required where nature of work allows employee to take intermittent rest periods equivalent to required standard. Director of Labor and*

Industries may grant variance from basic standard for good cause, upon employer application.

- *Although agricultural labor is excluded from the listed requirement of general application, a separate regulation requires a paid 10-minute rest period in each 4-hour period of agricultural employment.*

- *This jurisdiction also has meal period requirements.*

West Virginia

None

Wisconsin

None

Wyoming

None

APPENDIX 8 – EMPLOYMENT/ AGE CERTIFICATE OR "WORKING PAPER" REQUIREMENTS – JANUARY 1, 2013

This table includes both the general certification procedure required by law and those used in practice. Table does not include exceptions to the general procedures; nor does it identify certificates that may be required for employment in street trades, entertainment, or other work for which a special permit may be required.

Under the columns "For minors of age indicated" an entry of:

M denotes "Mandated," i.e., the requirement is mandated under State law;

R denotes on "Request," i.e., the certificate is not required under State law, but the law directs an administrative agency to issue the certificate on request;

P denotes "Practice," i.e., the law makes no requirement, but the State issues the certificate on request.
N/A indicates "not applicable." "No provision" as an entry under either employment or age certificate indicates that the issuance of such a certificate is unnecessary because another type of certificate covers all minors.

State	Type of Certificate Issued							
	Employment certificate			Age certification				
	For minors of age indicated	Issued by:		For minors of age indicated	Issued by:			
		Labor Department	School		Labor Department	School		
Alabama	Under 18 (M) 18 in mines No minor under 18 years of age may be employed in, about, or in connection with any of the following occupations, positions, or places: #3 In tunnels or excavations with depths exceeding four (4) feet. The following occupations in excavation operations are prohibited: Excavating, working in or backfilling (refilling) trenches, except manually excavating or manually backfilling trenches that do not exceed four feet in depth at any point. EXCEPTION - Minors age 16 or older may be issued a permit to work at excavation sites which are less than four (4) feet in depth.		X	Not issued				

State	Employment certificate			Age certification		
	For minors of age indicated	Issued by: Labor Department	Issued by: School	For minors of age indicated	Issued by: Labor Department	Issued by: School
Alaska	Under 17; Under 19 if employer licensed to sell alcohol (M)	X; In addition to individual certificates, employers may obtain advance approval for a specific job consisting of listed duties permitting them to hire minors, of at least 14 years of age, without prior individual approval.		Not issued		
Arizona	Not issued			Not issued		
Arkansas	Under 16 (M)	X		16 and 17 (P)	X	
California	Under 18 for minors enrolled in school (M)	X (for entertainment industry)	X	Not issued		

State	Type of Certificate Issued					
	Employment certificate			Age certification		
	For minors of age indicated	Issued by:		For minors of age indicated	Issued by:	
		Labor Department	School		Labor Department	School
Colorado	Under 16 during school hours (M)		X	Under 18 **except** not issued to minors under 16 during school hours (R)		X
Connecticut	Under 16 (M)		X	16 and 17 (M)		X
Delaware	Under 18 (M)	X	X	No provision		
District of Columbia	Under 18 (M)		X	No provision		
Florida	No provision			Under 18 (R) Employment or age certificates are not required. However, employers of any minor must obtain and keep on record proof of the child's age. An age certificate issued by the district school board is one method of meeting the proof of age requirement.		X

State	Type of Certificate Issued					
	Employment certificate			Age certification		
	For minors of age indicated	Issued by:		For minors of age indicated	Issued by:	
		Labor Department	School		Labor Department	School
Georgia	Under 18 (M)		X	No provision		
Guam	Under 16 (M)	X		Not issued		
Hawaii	Under 16 (M)	X		16 and 17 (M)	X	
Idaho	Not issued			Not issued		
Illinois	Under 16 (M)		X	16 to 20 (R)		X
Indiana	Under 18 (M)		X	18 to 21 (R)		X
Iowa	Under 16 (M)	Employment and age certificates are issued by both the Iowa Workforce Development Department and the schools.	X	16-18 and over (R)	Employment and age certificates are issued by both the Iowa Workforce Development Department and the schools.	X
Kansas	Under 16 and not enrolled in secondary school			Not issued		

State	Type of Certificate Issued					
	Employment certificate			Age certification		
	For minors of age indicated	Issued by:		For minors of age indicated	Issued by:	
		Labor Department	School		Labor Department	School
Kentucky	Not issued			Under 18(R)		X
Louisiana	Under 18 (M)		X	No provision		
Maine	Under 16 (M)	X		16 and 17 (R)	X	
Maryland	Under 18 (M)	X	X	No provision		
Massachusetts	Under 16 (M)		X	16 and 17 (M)		
Michigan	Under 18 (M)		X	No provision		

State	Type of Certificate Issued			Age certification		
	Employment certificate					
	For minors of age indicated	Issued by:		For minors of age indicated	Issued by:	
		Labor Department	School		Labor Department	School
Minnesota	Under 16 during school hours (M)		X	Under 18, **except** not issued to minors under 16 during school hours (R) — Age certificates are not required. However, employers of any minor must obtain and keep on record proof of the child's age. Age certificates satisfy this requirement as do copies of birth certificates, driver's licenses, and U.S. Department of Justice Immigration and Naturalization Service Employment Eligibility Verification Forms I-9.		X
Mississippi	Under 16 in mills, canneries, workshops, factories (M)		X	Not issued		
Missouri	Under 16 (M)		X	16 and over (R)		X

State	Type of Certificate Issued					
	Employment certificate			Age certification		
	For minors of age indicated	Issued by: Labor Department	School	For minors of age indicated	Issued by: Labor Department	School
Montana	Not issued. No certificate is required at any age in nonhazardous employment. Since minors under 16 may not work in hazardous employment, certificates for this age category are not deemed necessary.			16 and over: in hazardous occupations (M); in other occupations (R)	X	
Nebraska	Under 16 (M)		X	16 and over (R)		X
Nevada	Under 14 (M). Only certificates issued are those for minors under age 14 with written permission of district judge.			Not issued		

State	Employment certificate			Age certification		
	For minors of age indicated	Issued by: Labor Department	Issued by: School	For minors of age indicated	Issued by: Labor Department	Issued by: School
New Hampshire	Under 16 (M) Work certificates are not required for 16- and 17-year-olds. Instead, employers must maintain on file a signed, written document from the youth's parent or legal guardian authorizing the employment. The Department of Safety may issue age certificates to 16- and 17-year-olds.	X		Not issued		
New Jersey	Under 18 (M)		X	18 to 21 (R)		X
New Mexico	Under 16 (M)	X	X	16 and 17 (P)	X	X
New York	Under 18 (M)	X - for child performers	X	18 and over (P)		X

State	Type of Certificate Issued					
	Employment certificate			Age certification		
	For minors of age indicated	Issued by:		For minors of age indicated	Issued by:	
		Labor Department	School		Labor Department	School
North Carolina	Under 18 (M)	X	Employment certificates are issued by the Department of Labor or the County Director of Social Services.	No provision		
North Dakota	Under 16 (M)	X		16 and over (P)	X	
Ohio	Under 16 at any time, and 16 and 17 during school term (M)		X	Not issued. Age certificates are not issued, but proof of age is required for minors 16 and 17 years of age for employment during school vacation. With the approval of the Superintendent of Schools of the district where they live, 16- and 17-year-old minors are not required to provide a certificate to be employed at a seasonal amusement or recreational establishment.		

State	Employment certificate			Age certification		
	For minors of age indicated	Issued by: Labor Department	School	For minors of age indicated	Issued by: Labor Department	School
Oklahoma	Under 16 (M)		x	16 and 17 (P)		x
Oregon	Not issued. Minors age 14–17 are not required to obtain work permits. Instead, employers are required to apply for annual certificates to employ these minors.			No provision		
Pennsylvania	Under 18 (M)		X	No provision		
Puerto Rico	Under 18 (M)	X		18 to 21 (R)	X	
Rhode Island	Under 16 (M)		X	16 and 17 (M)		X
South Carolina	No provision			Under 18 (R). The State Department of Labor issues Federal age certificates upon request for minors under age 18.	X	

State	Employment certificate			Age certification		
	For minors of age indicated	Issued by: Labor Department	Issued by: School	For minors of age indicated	Issued by: Labor Department	Issued by: School
South Dakota	Not issued			Not issued		
Tennessee	Not issued No certificates are issued. However, employers of minors under age 18 must obtain and keep on file proof of the minor's age. A birth certificate, passport, driver's license, State issued identification, or parent's oath as to the minor's age are acceptable proofs of age under the child labor law.			Not issued No certificates are issued. However, employers of minors under age 18 must obtain and keep on file proof of the minor's age. A birth certificate, passport, driver's license, State issued identification, or parent's oath as to the minor's age are acceptable proofs of age under the child labor law.		
Texas	No provision			Under 18 (R)	X	

State	Type of Certificate Issued						
	Employment certificate			Age certification			
	For minors of age indicated	Issued by:		For minors of age indicated	Issued by:		
		Labor Department	School		Labor Department	School	
Utah	No provision			Under 18 (R)		X	
Vermont	Under 16 during school hours (M)	X		Not issued			
Virgin Islands	Under 18 (P)	X		No provision			
Virginia	Under 16 (M)		X	16 and 17 (R)		X	
Washington	Under 18 (M)	X		No provision			
West Virginia	Under 16 (M)		X	16 and 17 (R)		X	

State	Type of Certificate Issued						
	Employment certificate			Age certification			
	For minors of age indicated	Issued by:		For minors of age indicated	Issued by:		
		Labor Department	School		Labor Department	School	
Wisconsin	Under 18 (M)	X through permit officers Certificates are issued by volunteer permit officers who are representatives of the Department of Industry, Labor, and Human Relations. Many of the permit officers are school officials, but other public employees such as municipal and county employees and court officials are also included.		18 and over (R)	X through permit officers Certificates are issued by volunteer permit officers who are representatives of the Department of Industry, Labor, and Human Relations. Many of the permit officers are school officials, but other public employees such as municipal and county employees and court officials are also included.		
Wyoming	Not issued Employers of children under age 16 must maintain a proof of age.			Not issued			

APPENDIX 9 - MINIMUM WAGE LAWS BY STATES - JANUARY 1, 2013

The state minimum wage rate requirements, or lack thereof, are controlled by legislative activities within the individual states. Federal minimum wage law supersedes state minimum wage laws where the federal minimum wage is greater than the state minimum wage. In those states where the state minimum wage is greater than the federal minimum wage, the state minimum wage prevails.

There are four states than have a minimum wage set lower than the federal minimum wage. There are nineteen states (plus the District of Columbia) with minimum wage rates set higher than the federal minimum wage. There are twenty-two states that have a minimum wage requirement that is the same as the federal minimum wage requirement. The remaining five states do not have an established minimum wage requirement.

The State of Washington has the highest minimum wage at $9.19/hour. The states of Georgia and Wyoming have the lowest minimum wage ($5.15) of the 45 states that have a minimum wage requirement.

There are 10 states (Arizona, Colorado, Florida, Missouri, Montana, Nevada, Ohio, Oregon, Vermont, and Washington) that have minimum wages that are linked to a consumer price index. As a result of this linkage, the minimum wages in these states are normally increased each year, generally around January 1st. The exception is Nevada which adjusts the month of July each year. On January 1, 2013, there were nine of the ten states that increased their respective minimum wages. The exception was Nevada.

Like the Federal wage and hour law, State law often exempts particular occupations or industries from the minimum labor standard generally applied to covered employment. Particular exemptions are not identified in this table. Readers are encouraged to consult the laws of particular States in determining whether the State's minimum wage applies to a particular employment. This information often may be found at the websites maintained by State labor departments.

ALABAMA	Future Effective Date	Basic Minimum Rate (per hour)	Premium Pay After Designated Hours	
			Daily	Weekly
No state minimum wage law.				

ALASKA	Future Effective Date	Basic Minimum Rate (per hour)	Premium Pay After Designated Hours	
			Daily	Weekly
Under a voluntary flexible work hour plan approved by the Alaska Department of Labor, a 10 hour day, 40 hour workweek may be instituted with premium pay after 10 hours a day instead of after 8 hours. The premium overtime pay requirement on either a daily or weekly basis is not applicable to employers of fewer than 4 employees.		$7.75	8	40

ARIZONA	Future Effective Date	Basic Minimum Rate (per hour)	Premium Pay After Designated Hours	
			Daily	Weekly
Rate is increased annually based upon a cost of living formula.		$7.80		

ARKANSAS	Future Effective Date	Basic Minimum Rate (per hour)	Premium Pay After Designated Hours	
			Daily	Weekly
(Applicable to employers of 4 or more employees)		$6.25	N/A	40

CALIFORNIA	Future Effective Date	Basic Minimum Rate (per hour)	Premium Pay After Designated Hours	
			Daily	Weekly
Any work in excess of eight hours in one workday and any work in excess of 40 hours in one workweek and the first eight hours worked on the seventh day of work in any one workweek shall be at the rate of one and one-half times the regular rate of pay. Any work in excess of 12 hours in one day and any work in excess of eight hours on any seventh day of a workweek shall be paid no less than twice the regular rate of pay. California Labor Code section 310. Exceptions apply to an employee working pursuant to an alternative workweek adopted pursuant to applicable Labor Code sections and for time spent commuting. (See Labor Code sections 510 for exceptions).		$8.00	8, Over 12 (double time)	40; on 7th day: First 8 hours (time and half), Over 8 hours on 7th day (double time)

COLORADO	Future Effective Date	Basic Minimum Rate (per hour)	Premium Pay After Designated Hours	
			Daily	Weekly
Minimum wage rate and overtime provisions applicable to retail and service, commercial support service, food and beverage, and health and medical industries. Rate is increased or decreased annually based upon a cost of living formula.		$7.78	12	40

CONNECTICUT	Future Effective Date	Basic Minimum Rate (per hour)	Premium Pay After Designated Hours	
			Daily	Weekly
In restaurants and hotel restaurants, for the 7th consecutive day of work, premium pay is required at time and one half the minimum rate. The Connecticut minimum wage rate automatically increases to 1/2 of 1 percent above the rate set in the Fair Labor Standards Act if the Federal minimum wage rate equals or becomes higher than the State minimum.		$8.25		40

DELAWARE	Future Effective Date	Basic Minimum Rate (per hour)	Premium Pay After Designated Hours	
			Daily	Weekly
The Delaware minimum wage is automatically replaced with the Federal minimum wage rate if it is higher than the State minimum.		$7.25		

DISTRICT OF COLUMBIA	Future Effective Date	Basic Minimum Rate(per hour)	Premium Pay After Designated Hours	
			Daily	Weekly
In the District of Columbia, the rate is automatically set at $1 above the Federal minimum wage rate if the District of Columbia rate is lower.		$8.25		40

FLORIDA	Future Effective Date	Basic Minimum Rate(per hour)	Premium Pay After Designated Hours	
			Daily	Weekly
Rate is increased annually based upon a cost of living formula.		$7.79		N/A

GEORGIA	Future Effective Date	Basic Minimum Rate (per hour)	Premium Pay After Designated Hours	
			Daily	Weekly
(Applicable to employers of 6 or more employees) The State law excludes from coverage any employment that is subject to the Federal Fair Labor Standards Act when the Federal rate is greater than the State rate.		$5.15		

GUAM	Future Effective Date	Basic Minimum Rate (per hour)	Premium Pay After Designated Hours	
			Daily	Weekly
		$7.25		40

HAWAII	Future Effective Date	Basic Minimum Rate(per hour)	Premium Pay After Designated Hours	
			Daily	Weekly
An employee earning a guaranteed monthly compensation of $2,000 or more is exempt from the State minimum wage and overtime law. The State law excludes from coverage any employment that is subject to the Federal Fair Labor Standards Act unless the State wage rate is higher than the Federal.		$7.25		40

IDAHO	Future Effective Date	Basic Minimum Rate (per hour)	Premium Pay After Designated Hours	
			Daily	Weekly
		$7.25		

ILLINOIS	Future Effective Date	Basic Minimum Rate (per hour)	Premium Pay After Designated Hours [2]	
			Daily	Weekly
(Applicable to employers of 4 or more employees, excluding family members)		$8.25		40

INDIANA	Future Effective Date	Basic Minimum Rate(per hour)	Premium Pay After Designated Hours	
			Daily	Weekly
(Applicable to employers of 2 or more employees)		$7.25		40

IOWA	Future Effective Date	Basic Minimum Rate (per hour)	Premium Pay After Designated Hours	
			Daily	Weekly
The Iowa minimum wage is automatically replaced with the Federal minimum wage rate if it is higher than the State minimum.		$7.25		

KANSAS	Future Effective Date	Basic Minimum Rate(per hour)	Premium Pay After Designated Hours	
			Daily	Weekly
The State law excludes from coverage any employment that is subject to the Federal Fair Labor Standards Act.		$7.25		46

KENTUCKY	Future Effective Date	Basic Minimum Rate(per hour)	Premium Pay After Designated Hours	
			Daily	Weekly
The 7th day overtime law, which is separate from the minimum wage law differs in coverage from that in the minimum wage law and requires premium pay on the seventh day for those employees who work seven days in any one workweek. The state adopts the Federal minimum wage rate by reference if the Federal rate is greater than the State rate. Compensating time in lieu of overtime is allowed upon written request by an employee of any county, charter county, consolidated local government, or urban-county government, including an employee of a county-elected official.		$7.25		40 *7th day*

LOUISIANA	Future Effective Date	Basic Minimum Rate(per hour)	Premium Pay After Designated Hours	
			Daily	Weekly
There is no state minimum wage law.		N/A		N/A

MAINE	Future Effective Date	Basic Minimum Rate(per hour)	Premium Pay After Designated Hours	
			Daily	Weekly
The Maine minimum wage is automatically replaced with the Federal minimum wage rate if it is higher than the State minimum with the exception that any such increase is limited to no more than $1.00 per hour above the current legislated State rate.		$7.50		40

MARYLAND	Future Effective Date	Basic Minimum Rate(per hour)	Premium Pay After Designated Hours	
			Daily	Weekly
The Maryland minimum wage is automatically replaced with the Federal minimum wage rate if it is higher than the State minimum wage rate.		$7.25		40

MASSACHUSETTS	Future Effective Date	Basic Minimum Rate (per hour)	Premium Pay After Designated Hours	
			Daily	Weekly
The Massachusetts minimum wage rate automatically increases to 10 cents above the rate set in the Fair Labor Standards Act if the Federal minimum wage equals or becomes higher than the State minimum.		$8.00		40

MICHIGAN	Future Effective Date	Basic Minimum Rate (per hour)	Premium Pay After Designated Hours	
			Daily	Weekly
(Applicable to employers of 2 or more employees) The State law excludes from coverage any employment that is subject to the Federal Fair Labor Standards Act unless the State wage rate is higher than the Federal.		$7.40		40

MINNESOTA	Future Effective Date	Basic Minimum Rate(per hour)	Premium Pay After Designated Hours	
			Daily	Weekly
Large employer (enterprise with annual receipts of $625,000 or more)		$6.15		48
Small employer (enterprise with annual receipts of less than $625,000)		$5.25		48

MISSISSIPPI	Future Effective Date	Basic Minimum Rate (per hour)	Premium Pay After Designated Hours	
			Daily	Weekly
No state minimum wage law.		N/A		N/A

MISSOURI	Future Effective Date	Basic Minimum Rate (per hour)	Premium Pay After Designated Hours	
			Daily	Weekly
In addition to the exemption for federally covered employment, the law exempts, among others, employees of a retail or service business with gross annual sales or business done of less than $500,000. Premium pay required after 52 hours in seasonal amusement or recreation businesses. Minimum wage is to be increased or decreased by a cost of living factor starting January 1, 2008 and every January 1 thereafter.		$7.35		40

MONTANA	Future Effective Date	Basic Minimum Rate(per hour)	Premium Pay After Designated Hours	
			Daily	Weekly
Minimum wage is subject to a cost of living adjustment done by September 30 of each year and effective on January 1 of the following year State Law *Except businesses with gross annual sales of $110,000 or less*		$7.80		
Minimum wage is subject to a cost of living adjustment done by September 30 of each year and effective on January 1 of the following year		$4.00		40

NEBRASKA	Future Effective Date	Basic Minimum Rate(per hour)	Premium Pay After Designated Hours	
			Daily	Weekly
(Applicable to employers of 4 or more employees)		$7.25		

NEVADA	Future Effective Date	Basic Minimum Rate (per hour)	Premium Pay After Designated Hours	
			Daily	Weekly
The premium overtime pay requirement on either a daily or weekly basis is not applicable to employees who are compensated at not less than one and one-half times the minimum rate or to employees of enterprises having a gross annual sales volume of less than $250,000.

The minimum wage rate may be increased annually based upon changes in the cost of living index increase.

The premium overtime pay requirement on either a daily or weekly basis is not applicable to employees who are compensated at not less than one and one-half times the minimum rate or to employees of enterprises having a gross annual sales volume of less than $250,000.

The minimum wage rate may be increased annually based upon changes in the cost of living index increase. | | $8.25 (with no health ins. benefits provided by employer)

$7.25 (with health ins. benefits provided by employer and received by employee) | 8 | 40 |

NEW HAMPSHIRE	Future Effective Date	Basic Minimum Rate(per hour)	Premium Pay After Designated Hours	
			Daily	Weekly

The New Hampshire minimum wage is automatically replaced with the Federal minimum wage rate if it is higher than the State minimum.		$7.25		40

NEW JERSEY	Future Effective Date	Basic Minimum Rate(per hour)	Premium Pay After Designated Hours	
			Daily	Weekly
		$7.25		40

NEW MEXICO	Future Effective Date	Basic Minimum Rate(per hour)	Premium Pay After Designated Hours	
			Daily	Weekly
		$7.50		40

NEW YORK	Future Effective Date	Basic Minimum Rate(per hour)	Premium Pay After Designated Hours	
			Daily	Weekly
The New York minimum wage is automatically replaced with the Federal minimum wage rate if it is higher than the State minimum.		$7.25		40

NORTH CAROLINA	Future Effective Date	Basic Minimum Rate (per hour)	Premium Pay After Designated Hours	
			Daily	Weekly

Premium pay is required after 45 hours a week in seasonal amusements or recreational establishments.		$7.25		40

NORTH DAKOTA	Future Effective Date	Basic Minimum Rate(per hour)	Premium Pay After Designated Hours	
			Daily	Weekly
		$7.25		40

OHIO	Future Effective Date	Basic Minimum Rate(per hour)	Premium Pay After Designated Hours	
			Daily	Weekly
State Law		$7.85 $7.25 (for those employers grossing $283,000 or less)		40

OKLAHOMA	Future Effective Date	Basic Minimum Rate(per hour)	Premium Pay After Designated Hours	
			Daily	Weekly
Employers of ten or more full time employees at any one location and employers with annual gross sales over $100,000 irrespective of number of full time employees. The Oklahoma state minimum wage law does not contain current dollar minimums. Instead the state adopts the Federal minimum wage rate by reference. The State law excludes from coverage any employment that is subject to the Federal Fair Labor Standards Act. All other employers. The Oklahoma state minimum wage law does not contain current dollar minimums. Instead the state adopts the Federal minimum wage rate by reference. The State law excludes from coverage any employment that is subject to the Federal Fair Labor Standards Act.		$7.25 $2.00		

OREGON	Future Effective Date	Basic Minimum Rate (per hour)	Premium Pay After Designated Hours	
			Daily	Weekly
Premium pay required after 10 hours a day in nonfarm canneries, driers, or packing plants and in mills, factories or manufacturing establishments (excluding sawmills, planning mills, shingle mills, and logging camps). Beginning January 1, 2004, and annually thereafter, the rate will be adjusted for inflation by a calculation using the U.S. City Average Consumer Price Index for All Urban Consumers for All Items. The wage amount established will be rounded to the nearest five cents.		$8.95		40

PENNSYLVANIA	Future Effective Date	Basic Minimum Rate (per hour)	Premium Pay After Designated Hours	
			Daily	Weekly
		$7.25		40

PUERTO RICO	Future Effective Date	Basic Minimum Rate(per hour)	Premium Pay After Designated Hours	
			Daily	Weekly
Employers covered by the Federal Fair Labor Standards Act (FLSA) are subject only to the Federal minimum wage and all applicable regulations. Employers not covered by the FLSA will be subject to a minimum wage that is at least 70 percent of the Federal minimum wage or the applicable mandatory decree rate, whichever is higher. The Secretary of Labor and Human Resources may authorize a rate based on a lower percentage for any employer who can show that implementation of the 70 percent rate would substantially curtail employment in that business.		$7.25/hour for employees covered by the FLSA $5.08/hour for employees not covered by the FLSA	8 *And on statutory rest day (double time)*	40 *(double time)*

RHODE ISLAND	Future Effective Date	Basic Minimum Rate(per hour)	Premium Pay After Designated Hours	
			Daily	Weekly
Time and one-half premium pay for work on Sundays and holidays in retail and certain other businesses is required under two laws that are separate from the minimum wage law.		$7.75		40

SOUTH CAROLINA	Future Effective Date	Basic Minimum Rate(per hour)	Premium Pay After Designated Hours	
			Daily	Weekly
No state minimum wage law.		N/A		N/A

SOUTH DAKOTA	Future Effective Date	Basic Minimum Rate(per hour)	Premium Pay After Designated Hours	
			Daily	Weekly
		$7.25		

TENNESSEE	Future Effective Date	Basic Minimum Rate (per hour)	Premium Pay After Designated Hours	
			Daily	Weekly
No state minimum wage law. The state does have a promised wage law whereby the employers are responsible for paying to the employees the wages promised by the employer.		N/A		N/A

TEXAS	Future Effective Date	Basic Minimum Rate(per hour)	Premium Pay After Designated Hours	
			Daily	Weekly
The State law excludes from coverage any employment that is subject to the Federal Fair Labor Standards Act. The Texas State minimum wage law does not contain current dollar minimums. Instead the State adopts the Federal minimum wage rate by reference.		$7.25		

UTAH	Future Effective Date	Basic Minimum Rate (per hour)	Premium Pay After Designated Hours	
			Daily	Weekly
The Utah state minimum wage law does not contain current dollar minimums. Instead the state law authorizes the adoption of the Federal minimum wage rate via administrative action. The State law excludes from coverage any employment that is subject to the Federal Fair Labor Standards Act.		$7.25		

VERMONT	Future Effective Date	Basic Minimum Rate(per hour)	Premium Pay After Designated Hours	
			Daily	Weekly
(Applicable to employers of two or more employees) The State overtime pay provision has very limited application because it exempts numerous types of establishments, such as retail and service; seasonal amusement/recreation; hotels, motels, restaurants; and transportation employees to whom the Federal (FLSA) overtime provision does not apply. The Vermont minimum wage is automatically replaced with the Federal minimum wage rate if it is higher than the State minimum. Beginning January 1, 2007, and on each subsequent January 1, the minimum wage rate shall be increased by five percent or the percentage increase of the Consumer Price Index, or city average, not seasonally adjusted.		$8.60		40

VIRGINIA	Future Effective Date	Basic Minimum Rate(per hour)	Premium Pay After Designated Hours	
			Daily	Weekly
(Applicable to employers of 4 or more employees) The Virginia state minimum wage law does not contain current dollar minimums. Instead the state adopts the Federal minimum wage rate by reference. The State law excludes from coverage any employment that is subject to the Federal Fair Labor Standards Act.		$7.25		

VIRGIN ISLANDS	Future Effective Date	Basic Minimum Rate(per hour)	Premium Pay After Designated Hours	
			Daily	Weekly
State law *Except businesses with gross annual receipts of less than $150,000.*		$7.25 $4.30	8	40 *On 6th and 7th consecutive days.*

WASHINGTON	Future Effective Date	Basic Minimum Rate(per hour)	Premium Pay After Designated Hours	
			Daily	Weekly
Premium pay not applicable to employees who request compensating time off in lieu of premium pay. Beginning January 1, 2001, and annually thereafter, the rate will be adjusted for inflation by a calculation using the consumer price index for urban wage earners and clerical workers for the prior year.		$9.19		40

WEST VIRGINIA	Future Effective Date	Basic Minimum Rate(per hour)	Premium Pay After Designated Hours	
			Daily	Weekly
(Applicable to employers of 6 or more employees at one location)		$7.25		40

WISCONSIN	Future Effective Date	Basic Minimum Rate(per hour)	Premium Pay After Designated Hours	
			Daily	Weekly
		$7.25		40

WYOMING	Future Effective Date	Basic Minimum Rate(per hour)	Premium Pay After Designated Hours	
			Daily	Weekly
		$5.15		